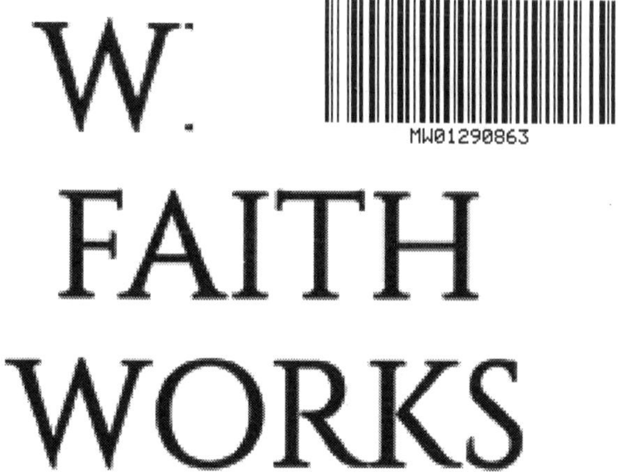

W
FAITH WORKS

LIVING OUT THE LAW OF LIBERTY ACCORDING TO JAMES

DAVID WILBER

When Faith Works: Living Out the Law of Liberty According to James

David Wilber
www.davidwilber.me

David has gone above and beyond in revealing just how vital the Book of James is for Christians today. Whether diving into James for an in-depth study or merely needing an easy-to-read commentary, you will be pleased to find what you are looking for in this book. However, the most impressive achievement that David has reached in this work is the convicting encouragement to walk outside one's home and transform the words of a 2,000 year old letter into action. I cannot imagine any believer being disappointed by adding this resource to their collection.

—**Matthew Vander Els,** Founded in Truth Ministries

A must read for every believer! David Wilber has delivered a keenly insightful examination of James' Epistle, connecting ancient Biblical wisdom with modern cultural relevancy. David's holistic approach confronts the pivotal questions every honest believer faces. Readers will be deeply inspired, as I was, to unshackle their faith by living out the Law of liberty.

—**Matthew Hoffmann**, Freedom Hill Community

David Wilber has produced a very readable book on a deplorably underemphasized topic within the sphere of modern Messianic teachings—namely, how to go beyond the bare bones of God's commandments into the realm of living as transformed creatures producing radically good fruit. Messiah came and told us that following a set of rules is next to meaningless unless our obedience springs from a place of genuine love for God and neighbor. I thoroughly enjoyed David's wonderful exploration of one of the most difficult discipleship manuals in Scripture—the Epistle of James. We would all do well to dive in ourselves and accept the challenge—nay, the imperative—to live by it.

—**Tyler Dawn Rosenquist**, Author of *The Bridge: Crossing Over into the Fullness of Covenant Life* and the *Context for Kids* curriculum series

After binge-reading this book, I could only appreciate how well every word of James was expounded upon and spoke so perfectly to all of us today in the faith. Every reader will find numerous instances of precious insight and well-needed reminders of what it means to be a Christian. James has always been a favorite of mine, and this book highlights every reason that the book of James is so fantastic.

—**Jon Sherman**, 119 Ministries

In his new book, *When Faith Works*, David Wilber examines James passage by passage and, in the process, illustrates two things about James beyond any doubt. First, James aligns perfectly with the rest of Scripture, both Old and New Testaments. Second, James is imminently relevant to the daily lives of believers in all nations, all cultures, and all strata of society. Whatever your pain, whatever your temptation, whatever your joy, James wrote for you. Wilber proves that James is among the most relevant, consistent, and impactful of all the Epistles. *When Faith Works* is a great book. I highly recommend it.

—**Jay Carper**, AmericanTorah

Reading through this book, one is left wondering whether it's a commentary on the book of James or a passionate letter from a friend about his love for God and the Scriptures. David takes a balanced look at the book of James, calling on modern scholarship and a theological search for the truth of God's Word. With a focus on the context of James within the entire Bible, this theological commentary is begging to encourage any who choose to read it, and it now has a permanent place in my library.

—**Matt Nappier** (MA in Old Testament), Beit Shalom Messianic Congregation

WHEN FAITH WORKS

LIVING OUT THE LAW OF LIBERTY ACCORDING TO JAMES

DAVID WILBER

But the one who looks into the perfect law, the law of liberty, and perseveres, being no hearer who forgets but a doer who acts, he will be blessed in his doing.
James 1:25

CONTENTS

PREFACE

How are we to live as followers of Yeshua?[1] How do we practically walk out our faith and devotion to God day by day? Why does God allow us to suffer, and what are we supposed to learn from our suffering? How do we overcome sin in our lives? What's the cause of conflict within our communities, and how do we resolve it? How do we make a difference in the world for Messiah's Kingdom? James' letter to early followers of Yeshua was written to address these questions, and the Spirit-inspired wisdom contained in this ancient epistle still speaks directly to us today.

Indeed, just as it was in the first century, many people today claim to be religious, but in reality their religion is "worthless" (James 1:26). Many people claim to have genuine faith, but in reality their faith is "dead" (James 2:17). Many people claim to be wise, but in reality their wisdom is "earthly, unspiritual, demonic" (James 3:16). James exposes fake, lifeless religion and points us toward an authentic expression of worship and devotion to the Messiah—a faith that works.

So how *does* faith work? How do we live out the law of liberty? That's what this book seeks to help you understand. We will explore what it means to have an authentic religion, faith, and wisdom according to the very brother of Yeshua. I pray that you will find this study on the epistle of James encouraging in your walk with our great Lord and Savior, Yeshua the Messiah.

---

1 Throughout this book I will be referring to Jesus by His Hebrew name, Yeshua, except for when I quote other sources.

INTRODUCTION

WHO IS JAMES?

James, a servant of God and of the Lord Jesus Christ, To the twelve tribes in the Dispersion: Greetings.
James 1:1

In the New Testament, four different men are referred to as "James." Yeshua had two disciples named James: James the son of Zebedee and brother of John[1] and James the son of Alphaeus.[2] Another James mentioned is the father of Judas.[3] The fourth James we see is the brother of Yeshua.[4] Though scholars debate it, this James is the likeliest author of this epistle. Dr. Craig Keener observes that Yeshua's brother James is most likely to have been the only one with the status to address "the twelve tribes" and identify himself only as "James":

> James was a common name, and when one spoke of a less commonly recognized individual with a common name, one

---

1 This James became a disciple early in Yeshua's ministry. Before he was called, he was part of a fishing business with his father, John, Peter, and Andrew (Matt. 4:18-21). He and his brother John were nicknamed "sons of thunder" by Yeshua (Mark 3:17), perhaps because of their zeal. (This is demonstrated by their desire to "call fire down from heaven" to destroy a Samaritan village that had rejected Yeshua.) This James was among the few to witness Yeshua's transfiguration (Matt. 17:1), and he was also the first disciple of Yeshua to be martyred (Acts 12:2).

2 This James is identified as a disciple of Yeshua in Matthew 10:3 and Acts 1:13. Apart from the fact that he was a disciple, nothing else is said about him in the Scriptures.

3 This James is mentioned in Luke 6:16. Apart from this reference, nothing else is said about him.

4 Acts 12:17; 15:13-21; 21:17-26; 1 Corinthians 15:6; Galatians 2:9, 12.

> usually added a qualifying title. Moreover, it seems unlikely that a letter composed by a relatively unknown James would have achieved sufficiently wide circulation as to survive. Many of the views reflected here (e.g. Jas 2:14-26) are also consistent with our knowledge of the James respected by the Jerusalem church (cf. Ac 21:18-25; Gal 2:10, 12).[5]

The name James comes from the Greek name *Iakōbos*, which is a transliteration of the Hebrew name *Ya'akov*, Jacob. Some scholars have argued that this name is properly translated into English as Jacob but was corrupted as it passed from Hebrew to Greek to Latin to English, ultimately morphing into James.[6] A popular assertion on the Internet is that King James had the book of James named after him instead of it being translated correctly into Jacob, but this has been thoroughly debunked.[7] In any case, James was known as *Ya'akov* in Jerusalem but referred to himself as *Iakōbos* when he interacted with Greek speakers.

James introduces himself as a servant of God and of the Lord Yeshua the Messiah. In addition, we know that James was the brother (technically the half-brother) of Yeshua, the son of Joseph and Mary, and the brother of Joseph, Simon, and Jude (Matthew 13:55; Jude 1). He did not believe in Yeshua during His early ministry (John 7:5) but later became a believer after being one of the select individuals to whom the resurrected Messiah appeared (1 Corinthians 15:7).

---

5 Craig Keener, *NIV Cultural Backgrounds Study Bible: Bringing to Life the Ancient World of Scripture*, James: "Authorship" (Grand Rapids, MI: Zondervan, 2016)

6 Dr. Michael Brown, Charisma News. "Recovering the Lost Letter of Jacob." www.charismanews.com. Accessed 8/5/18

7 The 1560 Geneva Version of the Bible has his name as Iames ("James" in modern English). This translation was published six years before King James was even born.

The apostle Paul considered James to be a "pillar" within the early Messianic community (Galatians 2:9).

James was a very influential figure in the early Messianic community. He presided over the Jerusalem Council during one of the most important theological questions addressed in the New Testament writings—that is, what are the spiritual status and requirements of Gentile followers of Messiah in the broader Messianic community? Some Pharisees taught that Gentile followers of Messiah needed to be circumcised—that is, formally convert to Judaism—in order to be "saved" (Acts 15:1).[8] The apostles argued that Gentiles are saved the same way Jews are saved—that is, by grace through faith in the Messiah (Acts 15:11). On the basis of biblical prophecy concerning Gentiles being included in God's plan of redemption (Acts 15:15-18; Amos 9:11-12), James ruled that it wasn't necessary for the Gentiles to "become Jewish" through ritual conversion in order to be included in the community of Messiah followers (Acts 15:19). However, in order to demonstrate to the broader Jewish community that the Gentiles had completely renounced their former idolatry, James ruled that they must strictly adhere to four prohibitions governing idol worship (Acts 15:20). Importantly, this ruling did not entail that Gentile believers

---

8 See Tim Hegg, *The Letter Writer: Paul's Background and Torah Perspective,* (Tacoma, WA: TorahResource, 2008): "The Jerusalem Council in Acts 15 was dealing with a specific issue: was it necessary for Gentiles to become proselytes and thus take on the full weight of the man-made laws of the Sages in order to be accepted within the Jewish community? The Council voiced a unified 'no' to this question. Using 'circumcision' as a short-hand designation for 'the ritual of becoming a proselyte,' the Council determined that the Gentiles would not need to be circumcised (i.e., become proselytes) in order to be received into the Torah community" (pp. 258-259).

were excused from Torah[9] observance beyond those four prohibitions. This is evident in the very next verse when we see that James had an expectation that the Gentiles would attend the synagogue and learn from the Torah every Sabbath (Acts 15:21).

James' commitment to the Torah is demonstrated further as we get to Acts 21:17-26. He was concerned about false rumors being spread among the Jewish community in Jerusalem claiming that the apostle Paul taught against the commandments of the Torah. Thus, James instructed Paul to assist a group of men in completing their Nazarite Vow[10] in order to prove that the rumors were untrue and that Paul in fact lived in accordance with the Torah. Just like Messiah Yeshua, who emphatically declared that the Torah has ongoing authority in lives of His followers (Matthew 5:17-20), James didn't want there to be the slightest misunderstanding about the validity of the Torah. From James' perspective, the Torah remained binding and authoritative.

Tradition holds that James was known for his extreme piety and righteousness and thus was surnamed "James the Just." It is said he prayed so often that his knees had large and thick calluses, making them look like camel knees.[11] According to the first century Jewish historian, Josephus, James was martyred around 62 AD. Josephus records that when a successor of Pilate, Festus, died in the AD 60s, the high priest Ananus II seized the opportunity to sentence James and

---

9 The Torah (often translated as "Law" in English) is a Hebrew word meaning "instructions, teaching." It often refers to the Pentateuch—that is, the first five books of the Bible—and contains God's commandments to His people as given through Moses.

10 In Acts 18:18, we see that Paul himself had perhaps taken a Nazarite Vow. For the laws concerning the Nazarite Vow, see Numbers 6.

11 Eusebius of Caesarea, *Ecclesiastical History*, trans. C.F. Cruse (Peabody, MA: Hendrickson, 1998), pp. 59-60

others to death by stoning.[12] Another account of James' death comes from Eusebius. He describes that a number of priests and Pharisees murdered James with stones and a club because of his faith in Yeshua. As he was being beaten to death, it is said that he, just like Yeshua, prayed that God would forgive his murderers.[13]

In summary, based on what we know from Scripture and tradition, James was a devout Jew, fully committed to the Messiah Yeshua. He had significant influence in the early Messianic and Jewish community. He was faithful to the Torah of Moses. And as we'll see throughout his epistle, he was highly concerned with justice, righteousness, and fidelity to God.

Who Are the Recipients?

James addressed his letter to "the twelve tribes in the Dispersion" (James 1:1)—that is, Jewish believers in Yeshua who had been scattered outside Palestine, perhaps due to persecution under Herod Agrippa I (Acts 12). Thus, scholars have suggested that James' epistle can be reliably dated between 44-49 A.D., making it the earliest written book of the New Testament.[14] In either case, James' audience is specifically made up of those who have already come to faith in Yeshua. This is clear by his specific mention of their faith in Messiah (James 2:1). Therefore, his focus throughout the epistle is to encourage his readers to make sure they are actually living in accordance to what they profess to believe.

Since this letter was written primarily to Jewish followers of Yeshua, it's not surprising that it is very Jewish in nature. In fact, the

---

12 Flavius Josephus, *Antiquities of the Jews*, 20.9.1 (Translated by William Whiston, 2017)

13 Eusebius of Caesarea: *Ecclesiastical History, trans. C.F. Cruse* (Peabody, MA: Hendrickson, 1998), pp. 60-61

14 John MacArthur, *Grace to You*. "Bible Introductions: James." www.gty.org. Accessed 8/5/18

"assembly" referenced in James 2:2 is the Greek word *synagoges*, which is translated as "Synagogue" everywhere else in the New Testament. Thus, James was writing to believers in Yeshua whose meetings took place in the synagogue. Moreover, the letter has an abundance of allusions to the *Tanakh*,[15] which of course would have been especially meaningful to a Jewish audience. Some scholars have even suggested that the epistle of James is essentially a verse-by-verse commentary on Leviticus 19.[16] Here are some of the significant parallels between James and Leviticus 19:

Leviticus 19	James
You shall not swear by my name falsely, and so profane the name of your God: I am the Lord. (Leviticus 19:12)	But above all, my brothers, do not swear, either by heaven or by earth or by any other oath, but let your "yes" be yes and your "no" be no, so that you may not fall under condemnation. (James 5:12)
You shall not oppress your neighbor or rob him. The wages of a hired worker shall not remain with you all night until the morning. (Leviticus 19:13)	Behold, the wages of the laborers who mowed your fields, which you kept back by fraud, are crying out against you, and the cries of the harvesters have reached the ears of the Lord of hosts. (James 5:4)

15 *Tanakh* is an acronym made up of the first Hebrew letter of each of the three subdivisions that make up the Hebrew Scriptures—*Torah* ("Instructions," or the five Books of Moses), *Nevi'im* ("Prophets"), and *Ketuvim* ("Writings").

16 Walter C. Kaiser, The Promise-Plan of God: A Biblical Theology of the Old and New Testaments (Grand Rapids, MI: Zondervan, 2008. EPUB: Ch. 12, para 20)

You shall do no injustice in court. You shall not be partial to the poor or defer to the great, but in righteousness shall you judge your neighbor. (Leviticus 19:15)	My brothers, show no partiality as you hold the faith in our Lord Jesus Christ, the Lord of glory. (James 2:1)
You shall not go around as a slanderer among your people, and you shall not stand up against the life of your neighbor: I am the Lord. (Leviticus 19:16)	Do not speak evil against one another, brothers. The one who speaks against a brother or judges his brother, speaks evil against the law and judges the law. But if you judge the law, you are not a doer of the law but a judge. (James 4:11)
You shall not hate your brother in your heart, but you shall reason frankly with your neighbor, lest you incur sin because of him. (Leviticus 19:17)	Let him know that whoever brings back a sinner from his wandering will save his soul from death and will cover a multitude of sins. (James 5:20)
You shall not take vengeance or bear a grudge against the sons of your own people, but you shall love your neighbor as yourself: I am the Lord. (Leviticus 19:18)	If you really fulfill the royal law according to Scripture, "You shall love your neighbor as yourself," you are doing well. (James 2:8)

There's no question that James highly regarded the Torah and affirmed its ongoing validity and authority in the lives of Yeshua's disciples, hence his use of the Torah as the basis for his teachings. James expounded on the commands of the Torah and taught their proper application within the context of the first century community of Messiah followers in light of the New Covenant. This is not unlike Yeshua's Sermon on the Mount. In fact, Yeshua's teachings, specifically

His Sermon on the Mount, likewise find many parallels in the epistle of James.[17]

While the primary recipients of James' letter were Jewish followers of Yeshua, Gentiles may also have been included within James' original audience. We know from the book of Acts that some Gentiles were coming to faith in Yeshua even before Paul was called to be an apostle to the Gentiles. Not only that, but as J.K. McKee suggests, the identity of the recipients of James' letter as "the twelve tribes" can perhaps take on an eschatological dynamic to include Gentile believers. The prophets in the *Tanakh* speak of a restored people of Israel in the last days who are identified as "the twelve tribes" and who also specifically include Gentiles among them (Ezekiel 47:21-23). McKee writes:

> If this factor bears some merit, then God's restored people in the eschaton is to include all Twelve Tribes of Israel recognizable (Isaiah 11:11-16; Zechariah 10:6-12), and concurrent with this, incorporate the righteous from the nations into an

---

17 *ESV Study Bible*, "Echoes of Jesus' Sermon on the Mount in James" (www.esv.org): Joy amid trials (Matt. 5:10-12; James 1:2); exhortation to be perfect (Matt. 5:48; James 1:4); asking God for good things (Matt. 7:7-11; James 1:5); God the giver of the good (Matt. 7:11; James 1:17); against anger (Matt 5:22; James 1:20); hearers and doers of the word (Matt. 7:24-27; James 1:22); poor inherit the kingdom (Matt. 2:5; James 5:3, 5); keeping the whole law (Matt 5:19; James 2:10); merciful receive mercy (Matt. 5:7; James 2:13); know them by their fruits (Matt. 7:16; James 3:12); blessings of peacemakers (Matt 5:9; James 3:18); ask and you will receive (Matt. 7:7-8; James 4:2-3); serving God vs. friendship with the world (Matt. 6:24; James 4:4); consolation for mourners (Matt. 5:4; James 4:9-10); against judging others (Matt. 7:1-5; James 4:11-12); living for today (Matt. 6:34; 4:13-14); moth and rust spoiling earthly treasures (Matt. 6:19; James 5:2-5); prophets as examples and patterns (Matt. 5:12; James 5:10); against oaths (Matt. 5:33-37; James 5:12).

expanded Kingdom realm of Israel, as James testified in Acts 15:15-18 (cf. Amos 9:11-12, LXX).[18]

James often refers to his audience as "brothers," appealing to them as family members in the faith. His audience is well-acquainted with suffering, injustice, and persecution, which accounts for James' teachings on steadfastness in the midst of trials. As a leader within the early Messianic community, James wrote with the goal of encouraging a dispersed people who were facing extreme difficulties.

What is the Theme?

James emphasizes the practical side of faith. He exhorts his audience to be uncompromisingly devoted to God and to demonstrate their faith by their behavior. The epistle of James is similar to the wisdom literature of the *Tanakh* (Proverbs, Ecclesiastes, etc.) with its emphasis on wise living. James unpacks the importance of remaining steadfast in the midst of trials, doing good works, responding to conflict with patience, and rejecting worldliness and hypocrisy. In short, as the brother of Yeshua, James teaches us what it means to have an authentic faith that works.

18 J.K. McKee, *James for the Practical Messianic* (Richardson, TX: Messianic Apologetics, 2013), p. 9

CHAPTER 1

REJOICE IN SUFFERING

Count it all joy, my brothers, when you meet trials of various kinds, for you know that the testing of your faith produces steadfastness. And let steadfastness have its full effect, that you may be perfect and complete, lacking in nothing.

James 1:2-4

The first instruction James gives his readers is to consider trials to be a joy. Why? The simple answer, according to James, is that God uses trials for our benefit. Christian scholar Scot McKnight says, "To consider trials as an occasion of joy involves an act of faith, for instead of looking at the trial, the messianic Jewish community is instead encouraged to look *through* the trial to its potential outcome."[1] How are trials beneficial? What good can come out of things like poverty, temptation, loss, suffering, injustice, and persecution? James says that these trials we endure as believers refine our faith and bring us to a place of spiritual maturity—that we may be "perfect and complete, lacking in nothing" (v. 4). This doesn't mean being sinless, but James expects his readers to grow in godly character consistent with the standards of God's perfect Word. Paul makes a similar statement in Romans:

> Not only that, but we rejoice in our sufferings, knowing that suffering produces endurance, and endurance produces character, and character produces hope. (Romans 5:3)

---

1 Scot McKnight, *The New International Commentary of the New Testament: The Letter of James* (Grand Rapids, MI: Wm. B. Eerdmans Publishing, 2011) p. 71

This is a difficult instruction. How do we rejoice in our suffering? After all, nobody in their right mind enjoys having to endure trials, pain, and persecution. The thought of considering times of suffering to be "joyful" occasions is counterintuitive. Not only that, but the reality of suffering in our world is perhaps the biggest obstacle to having faith in an all-loving God. Believers and unbelievers alike often ask, "If God loves us, why would He allow us to experience such pain?" To truly appreciate and be able to apply this instruction from James, we need to look at how the Bible broadly answers the problem of suffering.

God and the Problem of Evil and Suffering

The problem of evil and suffering is not merely an academic or theoretical question. It's a reality that affects all of us in a deeply personal way. Indeed, we personally endure various types of suffering all the time. For instance, perhaps no experience is more painful and devastating than losing a loved one to death. And yet, this is a difficult road most of us find ourselves having to navigate at times in our lives. When we lose someone we love, like a child or friend or our spouse, and we're faced with that paralyzing grief, it's hard not to be angry at God or to question whether He even exists. Another type of suffering that we experience is sickness and disease. Even if we have not had to deal with it ourselves, we likely know people who live with chronic pain, and often we're moved by compassion to ask the Lord, "Why must this person live in pain? Why don't You just heal them?" Additionally, we witness the suffering of others due to injustice and oppression. We see it all the time—abortion, sex trafficking, racism, rape, child abuse. As we observe the suffering in the world due to the sheer evil residing in the hearts of mankind, we're often left in a state of complete bewilderment.

Many of us have friends or acquaintances who've said they cannot believe in God because of the evil and suffering in the world. Maybe you've felt that way yourself. The pain we've seen and experienced, even as Christians, may make us struggle to believe that God is involved or that He cares about us. How can a God who supposedly loves people allow such evil and suffering to continue? This is an important question we need to wrestle with. Thankfully, the Bible is not silent on this issue.

In this chapter, we will answer four questions relating to the problem of suffering:

1) Does the reality of suffering disprove God's existence?
2) Why do bad things happen to good people?
3) What are God's answers to the problem of suffering?
4) How are we to respond to the suffering in our world?

The answers given here are by no means a full treatment of the issue.[2] However, having a basic understanding of how to answer these important questions will help us better appreciate and apply James' instruction to "count it all joy" when we are faced with trials.

A common objection you'll hear from atheists might go something like this: "There cannot be a God because there's too much evil and suffering in the world." The atheists I've had conversations with have raised this objection more times than I can count. And I have to admit, from an emotional standpoint, this is a powerful objection. Emotionally, it's oftentimes difficult to believe in a God who has the power to intervene and yet allows a child to die of cancer or a young woman to be raped and murdered. However, when we examine this objection

---

2 For a fuller treatment, I recommend the relevant chapters in Dr. William Lane Craig's book, *Hard Questions, Real Answers*.

logically, it breaks down. In fact, ironically, the reality of evil and suffering makes more sense with a theistic worldview than with an atheistic worldview. That is to say, theism—biblical Christianity in particular—gives us the best philosophical framework for understanding why evil and suffering exist and how we can address it.

First of all, when it comes to morality, the existence of evil entails the existence of good. Second, the existence of good and evil entails the existence of a transcendent moral law by which good and evil can be identified. (Otherwise "good" and "evil" would not be objectively real.) Third, the existence of a transcendent moral law entails the existence of a transcendent moral law giver—also known as God. Here is how professor of philosophy, Peter Kreeft, puts it:

> What are moral laws? Unlike the laws of physics or the laws of mathematics, which tell us what is, the laws of morality tell us what ought to be. But like physical laws, they direct and order something. And that something is right human behavior. But since morality doesn't exist physically—there are no moral or immoral atoms, or cells or genes—its cause has to be something that exists apart from the physical world. That thing must therefore be above nature—or super-natural. The very existence of morality proves the existence of something beyond nature and beyond man. Just as a design suggests a designer, moral commands suggest a moral commander.[3]

Indeed, the argument against God's existence on the basis of evil breaks down because you have to assume God's existence in order to

---

3 Peter Kreeft, *Prager University*. "Where Do Good and Evil Come From?" www.prageru.com. Accessed 8/15/2018

even make the objection. Without God, the most that we can say when terrible acts are committed, such as the Holocaust or slavery, is that we personally don't like it, but we cannot call them what they truly are—evil. Why? Because we cannot judge something to be evil without an objective standard, and the only way that standard can exist is if God exists. Thus, without God, the very objection on the basis of evil and suffering is meaningless. Only if God exists can we discuss the problem of evil and suffering in a meaningful way.

Now we get to an even bigger question: Why do bad things happen to good people? We've established that the existence of evil and suffering is not incompatible with the existence of God. In fact, the only way "good" and "evil" can truly exist is if God exists. But how can God be *all-good* and still permit the evil and suffering in our world? If God is all-good, shouldn't we expect that He would intervene and put an end to evil and suffering? Though the reality of evil and suffering doesn't disprove the existence of God, surely it proves that He's not all-good, right?

This objection can be answered in a couple of ways. The first answer is that God gave humans the ability to choose whether to do good or evil. God's desire is that humans would choose to do good. As Moses commanded, "Choose life, that you and your offspring may live" (Deuteronomy 30:19). But we often choose to go against God's will by doing evil. Instead of choosing life, we choose death. Instead of choosing love and blessings, we choose to do things that hurt ourselves and others. In fact, the very reason we wrestle with this question of evil and suffering to begin with is because of Adam's choice to disobey God and pursue what was contrary to God's will. The apostle Paul says that sin entered the world through one man, and with sin came death, sorrow, and suffering (Romans 5:12). This is the world we've inherited because of the choice that Adam made. But it wasn't just Adam who made that choice to eat from the tree of knowledge—we all have. The Bible says that we all have sinned (Romans 3:23). Every time we lie to someone, steal from them, betray them, we are taking a bite out of that forbidden fruit just as Adam did. We have all chosen death over life. And indeed, we must come to grips with the fact that much of the human suffering in our world is the result of human choices to do evil. But the fact that humans choose to do evil does not prove that God isn't good.

Someone might say, "That's fine, but what about seemingly senseless suffering that doesn't appear to be the direct result of human choices?" Well, another way that we might make some sense of God's goodness in light of suffering is by the fact that God is all-knowing and sees the end from the beginning. But we, as finite creatures, have limited knowledge of the universe and God's plans. We therefore cannot judge God as having no good reason for allowing suffering. To put it another way, the burden of proof is on the person making the objection to show that evil and suffering are logically incompatible with an all-good God. But as long as it's *possible* that God has good reasons for allowing evil and suffering, the objection breaks down. The atheist must prove that it is *impossible* for God to have good reasons for allowing evil and suffering to continue. However, since we are not omniscient, we simply aren't in a position to be able to prove such a claim. Christian philosopher, William Lane Craig, puts it this way:

> Evils which appear pointless to us within our limited framework may be seen to have been justly permitted within God's wider framework. To borrow an illustration from a developing field of science, Chaos Theory, scientists have discovered that certain macroscopic systems, for example, whether systems or insect populations, are extraordinarily

> sensitive to the tiniest perturbations. A butterfly fluttering on a branch in West Africa may set in motion forces which would eventually issue in a hurricane over the Atlantic Ocean. Yet it is impossible in principle for anyone observing that butterfly palpitating on a branch to predict such an outcome. The brutal murder of an innocent man or a child's dying of leukemia could produce a sort of ripple effect through history such that God's morally sufficient reason for permitting it might not emerge until centuries later and perhaps in another land.[4]

Due to our limited knowledge, we simply cannot judge whether or not God has good reasons for allowing evil and suffering. However, as followers of Yeshua, we can have faith that God *does* have good reasons because we know that God is good. We know that He is perfectly just, and we can trust that His ways are righteous even if we don't see it from our finite perspectives. And this isn't blind faith—many of us have experienced this in our own lives! We remember certain tragedies and difficulties we've had to endure, and we can look back and see God's good purpose in allowing us to go through them.

A good example of this in Scripture is Jacob's son, Joseph. The story begins with God giving Joseph all of these amazing dreams and promises. Shortly thereafter, he was betrayed by his own family, thrown into a well, sold into slavery, and then later put into prison falsely accused. You could probably imagine how Joseph felt as he went through these various hardships: "God, I thought you gave me all of these amazing promises! I thought you had this great plan for my life! Why would you allow me to go through all of this?" Little did Joseph know at the time

---

4 William Lane Craig, *Reasonable Faith*. "The Problem of Evil." www.reasonablefaith.org. Accessed 6/15/2018

that God allowed him to go through those difficulties in order to put him in the position to fulfill the very promises God gave Him. Had Joseph not gone through the series of painful events that eventually led to his being a prisoner in a foreign land, he wouldn't have had the opportunity to meet the Pharaoh and be made second in command over all of Egypt so that Israel could be saved from famine. As believers, we can trust that God has good reasons for allowing suffering even when it doesn't make sense from our limited perspectives.

Now that we've established that evil and suffering are not incompatible with God's existence or goodness, what are God's answers to this problem? Interestingly, while the problem of evil and suffering is perhaps the biggest obstacle to belief in God, the God of the Bible offers the only real solutions. We will unpack four answers in regard to this question.

The first answer to the problem of evil and suffering is that one day evil and suffering will end. Scripture teaches that one day in the future, Yeshua's kingdom will come to earth in fullness, and this will bring about a complete end to evil and suffering forever:

> And I saw the holy city, new Jerusalem, coming down out of heaven from God, prepared as a bride adorned for her husband. And I heard a loud voice from the throne saying, "Behold, the dwelling place of God is with man. He will dwell with them, and they will be his people, and God himself will be with them as their God. He will wipe away every tear from their eyes, and death shall be no more, neither shall there be mourning, nor crying, nor pain anymore, for the former things have passed away. (Revelation 21:2-4)

This passage from Revelation is a prophecy that takes place after Yeshua returns, after the millennial reign, when a new Jerusalem is ushered into our reality. The Lord promises that one day there won't be any more death, pain, or mourning. God will set all things right. If you remove God from the equation and therefore remove the reality of Yeshua's coming kingdom, suffering is never made right. There's never any justice or resolution. Innocent people suffer and evil prevails and that's it—that's what atheism gives us. But with God, we have hope. In fact, the reality of Yeshua's coming kingdom is such a wonderful promise that Paul compares the sufferings of this life to a "light momentary affliction" in light of the everlasting joy that awaits us (2 Corinthians 4:16-18).

Someone might ask, "Why can't God just abolish all suffering now? Why do we have to wait for this future kingdom to come?" The answer to that question lies with the Bible's second answer to the problem of suffering. But before we unpack that second answer, it's important that we address a popular false doctrine that has pervaded large segments of the Church. This false doctrine is the idea taught by "prosperity preachers" that the point of this life is to have health, wealth, and prosperity. In other words, God's job is to make sure that His little human creatures have nice, comfortable lives, and that God will magically make all their problems go away! If the Bible actually taught this idea (it doesn't), then I would agree with the atheist that suffering is pointless. But that isn't what the Bible teaches. The goal of this life is not to attain health, wealth, and prosperity, but to attain the knowledge of God and to bring Him glory. To that end, suffering is not pointless but is in fact an opportunity to fulfill the purpose of this life. And that brings us to the second answer to the problem of suffering: Redemption/Sanctification.

God works all things together for good, for those who are called according to His purpose (Romans 8:28). We often grow spiritually through suffering; we learn obedience and gain wisdom. As James puts it, our suffering produces steadfastness, which results in our becoming "perfect and complete, lacking in nothing" (James 1:4). The psalmist said, "Before I was afflicted I went astray, but now I keep your word" (Psalm 119:67). If it weren't for the suffering we've had to endure in life, we simply wouldn't be who we are today. According to Scripture, the only way to fulfill our purpose, reach spiritual maturity, and have true fulfillment is by knowing God and bringing Him glory in our lives—and that often comes through trials.

This brings us to our third answer to the problem of suffering: God. God understands our suffering. He's involved. He responds. God gives our suffering meaning. In the Bible, Job was a man who went through unfathomable suffering, and we clearly see that he—a mere man—was important enough to God that God drew near to him in his affliction. God answered Job. And yes, God gave a word of reproof to Job and his friends, but it's enough that God even answered at all. Think about it: He's the sovereign Creator and King of the Universe. He doesn't owe us anything, but He still chooses to respond to us in our affliction rather than letting us wallow in our misery. In addition to responding to us in our afflictions, God *understands* our deepest pain and sorrows. For instance, our Messiah, Yeshua Himself, was deeply affected by the pain of loss. The Scriptures record that He wept over the death of His friend Lazarus:

> When Jesus saw her weeping, and the Jews who had come with her also weeping, he was deeply moved in his spirit and greatly troubled. And he said, "Where have you laid him?"

> They said to him, "Lord, come and see." Jesus wept. So the Jews said, "See how he loved him!" (John 11:33-36)

"Jesus wept." What a profound statement! These two simple words speak volumes to the character and love of our Messiah. When Yeshua saw the pain of all those affected by the death of Lazarus, He was moved to the point of tears. What's amazing about this is that Yeshua already knew that Lazarus would soon be raised from the dead (John 11:11, 41-44). Knowing this, why did He weep? He wept, I believe, because He took on our sorrow as His own: "Surely he has borne our griefs and carried our sorrows" (Isaiah 53:4). Death is not the end for those who know Yeshua. Like Lazarus, those who have fallen asleep will rise again. A day will come when God will set everything right and wipe the tears from our eyes, and in that day death will be no more. But in the meantime, we can take comfort in the fact that God understands our pain. In our moments of immense grief and heartache, God is weeping with us. Scripture says that the Lord is near to the brokenhearted (Psalm 34:18). He has a special place in His heart for hurting people. Therefore, far from being pointless, suffering is an opportunity to worship God and experience His loving presence in a deep and profound way. Charles Spurgeon puts it well:

> Have you never known what it is, in times of peace and quietness, to feel as if you missed the grandeur of the presence of God? I have looked back to times of trial with a kind of longing, not to have them return, but to feel the strength of God as I have felt it then, to feel the power of faith, as I have

> felt it then, to hang upon God's powerful arm as I hung upon it then, and to see God at work as I saw him then.[5]

The last answer to the problem of suffering is this: Scripture teaches us that God desires to work through His people to relieve the suffering of the world. How do we do that? First, we must stop causing it. We must love our neighbor as ourselves. We must stop lying, stealing, and taking advantage of people. We must lay our lives down for others, even our enemies. Indeed, we are never going to resolve the problem of suffering by continuing to contribute to it through our own evil choices.

Second, we are to stand up against injustice. We are to actively visit and care for the sick, the poor, and the oppressed. We are not only to pray for people but also invest in their lives. Like Yeshua, we are to weep with those who weep (Romans 12:15). In Isaiah 58—a powerful chapter that outlines God's expectations of His people in bringing about His kingdom in this world—we are commanded to free the oppressed, share our food with the hungry, give shelter to the homeless, clothe the naked, meet the needs of the afflicted, etc., and then healing and restoration will break forth into the world.

Third, we must pray for physical, emotional, and spiritual healing. As Yeshua's disciples, we've been given authority to cast out demons and bring healing to the sick (Mark 16:17-18). We are to expect these manifestations of God's power as we walk in faith. We eagerly await the time when Yeshua's kingdom will arrive in fullness and suffering will end, but that doesn't mean we sit on our hands. As disciples of

---

5 Charles H. Spurgeon, Commentary on James 1:4. "Spurgeon's Verse Expositions of the Bible." www.studylight.org. Accessed 6/15/2018

Yeshua, we have an active role in bringing about God's rule on this earth in our present day.

Now that we have a fuller understanding of the Bible's answers to the problem of evil and suffering, we can better appreciate James' instruction to "count it all joy" when we are faced with trials. We know that the pain we see and experience is not incompatible with an all-loving God. We know that evil and death have been conquered at the cross and that one day suffering will be completely abolished. Moreover, we know that God is near to the brokenhearted. In the very depths of our despair, He holds us and weeps with us. Ultimately, we know that suffering has a redemptive side. God uses our suffering for our sanctification that we may become "perfect and complete, lacking in nothing" (James 1:4). We know that God's desire is to use us to bring life and healing to a hurting world. And since true fulfillment in this life comes only from knowing God, growing in our relationship with Him, and doing His will, we can therefore rejoice in the midst of trials.

CHAPTER 2

ASK FOR GOD'S WISDOM

If any of you lacks wisdom, let him ask God, who gives generously to all without reproach, and it will be given him. But let him ask in faith, with no doubting, for the one who doubts is like a wave of the sea that is driven and tossed by the wind. For that person must not suppose that he will receive anything from the Lord; he is a double-minded man, unstable in all his ways.

James 1:5-8

After James tells us to rejoice when our faith is tested by trials, he immediately speaks about our need for wisdom. He says if we lack wisdom, then we need to ask God for it. This exhortation seems somewhat disconnected from the previous passage, but James follows his remarks on remaining steadfast in the midst of trials with this call to seek God's wisdom for a reason. It goes back to reaching spiritual maturity—that is, becoming "perfect and complete, lacking in nothing." Having God's wisdom is essential to being joyful in the midst of trials, and being joyful in the midst of trials is essential to reaching spiritual maturity.

When a person who lacks God's wisdom experiences difficulties, they tend to react out of emotion. They let their fear or anger influence their decisions, which often leads to retaliation, division, and quarreling within the body of believers. Followers of Yeshua are not to be led by our emotions; we are to have self-control and navigate trials with patience and wisdom. That is to say, we are to try to see trials from God's perspective. Wisdom enables us to take a step back and see what God might be teaching us and how we might bring glory to His name in the midst of whatever we're going through.

James says that when we ask God for His wisdom, He gives generously without reproach. However, we must ask "in faith, with no doubting" (v. 6), otherwise we will not receive anything from God. Indeed, the one who doubts God is compared to a wave of the sea, driven and tossed by the wind. As Dr. Paul Copan points out,[1] this doubt that James speaks of is indicative of someone who is unstable and double-minded, which James later defines as having a mindset of divided allegiance between God and the world:

> You adulterous people! Do you not know that friendship with the world is enmity with God? [...] Cleanse your hands, you sinners, and purify your hearts, you double-minded. (James 4:4, 8)

In this context, doubt seems to connect back to spiritual immaturity and our inclination to be led by our emotions as opposed to remaining steadfast in our spiritual walk. Thus, James calls on us to be consistent and unwavering with regard to the wisdom that God reveals to us. In other words, when we ask for wisdom, we ask "in faith." And, as he unpacks later in this epistle, James' definition of faith necessarily results in works (2:14-26). Doubt, therefore, is the refusal to consistently walk out what God has revealed. Those who waver in their commitment to the Lord, "limping between two different opinions," as Elijah put it (1 Kings 18:21), will not receive anything from God. But those who remain steadfast in their commitment to God, especially in the midst of trials, will grow in maturity and wisdom.

---

1 Paul Copan, *A Little Book For New Philosophers* (Downers Grove, IL: IVP Academic of InterVarsity Press), p. 103

Dealing With Doubt

As we've already covered, the doubt that James speaks of is more of a failure to consistently live for God. James is not speaking of those with honest intellectual struggles in regard to their faith. However, many people have misunderstood this passage to be saying that all doubt is sinful. This misunderstanding has caused many believers to try to dismiss their inward struggles and questions rather than seeking resolution. Indeed, struggling believers are often told by other Christians to ignore their nagging doubts and "just believe." But this is the wrong response to intellectual doubt. James is not rebuking believers for having genuine struggles with difficult questions about God or particular biblical doctrines. James is rebuking hypocrisy and unfaithfulness. Even in the midst of intellectual doubt, believers can still faithfully serve and follow God.

Having said that, intellectual doubt is a concern that we should seek to resolve. While some believers pretend that their doubts don't exist, others seem to almost glorify their doubts. In both cases, doubt is never actually addressed and therefore could potentially lead to a deterioration of one's faith.

So how do we overcome doubt? First, we recognize that doubt is a condition of our humanity. We must choose to be honest about our doubts and take our struggles to God and the Church. Jude, the brother of James, instructs us to "have mercy on those who doubt" (Jude 22). Thus, the Church ought to be about the business of ministering to the doubtful. That means allowing those who have doubts the room to honestly wrestle with difficult questions while giving them guidance and working with them to find answers.

Second, we must search for answers to the topics that trouble us. Whether we're struggling with the existence of God, a doctrine or passage in the Bible that we find troubling, or whatever the topic may be, answers are available. Believers have been wrestling with every difficult question imaginable for thousands of years. Read books and watch videos from Christian apologists who have dedicated their lives to providing answers to these difficult questions. Don't give up wrestling with God until you are content in your mind with an answer.

Third, we must understand that doubt is not only an intellectual but also a spiritual matter. While we seek intellectual resolution for our doubts, we cannot neglect the spiritual aspect of the matter. Too often believers justify their abandonment of spiritual discipline—prayer, corporate worship, Bible reading, etc.—on the basis of their doubts. They say, "I feel like a hypocrite because of my intellectual struggles, so I will not pray or attend Church or Synagogue services until I overcome my doubts." But abandoning spiritual discipline when faced with doubts is a step in the wrong direction. It ultimately hinders the spiritual growth that comes through the struggle. This actually takes us right back to the overall theme that we've seen so far in James' epistle. When we remain steadfast in the midst of having our faith tested by trials—including when we're faced with doubt—we will grow in spiritual maturity. But again, we must remain steadfast in order to overcome doubt and achieve a deepened faith as a result.

CHAPTER 3

REMAIN STEADFAST

Let the lowly brother boast in his exaltation, and the rich in his humiliation, because like a flower of the grass he will pass away. For the sun rises with its scorching heat and withers the grass; its flower falls, and its beauty perishes. So also will the rich man fade away in the midst of his pursuits. Blessed is the man who remains steadfast under trial, for when he has stood the test he will receive the crown of life, which God has promised to those who love him.

James 1:9-12

James now addresses the issues of poverty and wealth. This passage seems a little out of place from what has come before, but it fits into James' overall argument in a couple of ways. First, poverty is a "trial" that tests our faith. This fact was especially relevant to James' original audience. The majority of his readers lived in poverty and were often oppressed by the rich. Due to the Roman general Pompey's siege of Jerusalem in 63 BC, many Jewish peasants were made landless. Moreover, small farmers were driven out of business due to the exorbitant taxes of Herod the Great.[1] As a result of not having their own land, Jewish peasants had to work as tenants on large, feudal estates or as day laborers in the marketplaces.[2] As for living conditions, Keener notes:

> The poor in Rome mostly lived in rickety tenements that often caught fire or collapsed; running water was not available above

---

1 Craig Keener, *NIV Cultural Backgrounds Study Bible: Bringing to Life the Ancient World of Scripture*, James: "Poverty and Revolt in Judea" (Grand Rapids, MI: Zondervan, 2016)

2 Ibid.

> the ground floor, and apartments on the highest floors were large enough only for sleeping. Conditions were also dismal for the poor in Jerusalem. Whereas the aristocracy lived in spacious homes in Jerusalem's upper city, the city's poor lived downwind of that City's sewers.[3]

Poor people in the first century didn't have many options. Add to their already distressing situation the fact that the rich persecuted them (James 2:6-7) and withheld their pay (James 5:4-6), it's easy to see why the relationship between the poor and the rich aristocracy was tense. But rather than retaliate with violence, James exhorts his readers to endure this trial with steadfastness and wisdom, seeing their current lowly situation from God's perspective. Indeed, while the rich might be comfortable in this life, this life is only temporary. As James says, it will all wither away like grass in the scorching heat. Therefore, from an eternal standpoint, the humble people of God who endure trials are the true wealthy people in the exalted position. God has chosen the poor to be rich in faith:

> Listen, my beloved brothers, has not God chosen those who are poor in the world to be rich in faith and heirs of the kingdom, which he has promised to those who love him? (James 2:5)

In fact, James calls these poor believers who endure trials "blessed," which is an idea he repeats in chapter 5:

---

3 Ibid.

> Behold, we consider those blessed who remained steadfast. You have heard of the steadfastness of Job, and you have seen the purpose of the Lord, how the Lord is compassionate and merciful. (James 5:11)

This blessing for faithful endurance has implications for both the present and future. In addition to becoming "perfect and complete" and fulfilling their destiny in this life by bringing about God's Kingdom on earth, faithful believers are promised a "crown of life" in the world to come (v. 12).[4] It should be noted that faithful endurance, to James, is not merely a mental affirmation of the truth of God and His promises, but something that impacts our behavior, as we'll see throughout the rest of his epistle.

The Sin of Comparison

It's a natural human inclination to look at the lives of people who appear to have it all together and wish we had what they had. However, this longing can often lead to bitterness and resentment toward God and our neighbor. Often when we aren't happy with our current circumstances in life, we act just like the Israelites in the wilderness who complained and grumbled and blamed God—even to the point of wanting to return to being enslaved in Egypt! Our desire to compare is ultimately rooted in covetousness, which is a violation of the Tenth Commandment:

---

4 This theme of believers receiving a crown in the world to come is echoed by Yeshua (Revelation 2:10) as well as Peter (1 Peter 5:4) and Paul (1 Corinthians 9:25; 2 Timothy 4:8)

> You shall not covet your neighbor's house; you shall not covet your neighbor's wife, or his male servant, or his female servant, or his ox, or his donkey, or anything that is your neighbor's. (Exodus 20:17)

We can understand this commandment as simply, "Do not yearn to have your neighbor's life instead of the life God gave you." Unlike most of the other commandments in the Torah, which are focused on prohibiting certain actions, the command not to covet focuses on prohibiting a certain attitude of the heart. In fact, James tells us that sin originates from our own heart's desires (James 1:15). Therefore, since coveting is a strong desire, it follows that many other sins—dishonesty, theft, adultery, even murder—are birthed from covetousness.

When we break the Tenth Commandment, we also break the two greatest commandments to love God and love our neighbor (Matthew 22:34-40). Covetousness breaks the command to love God by telling Him that He and the blessings He's given us are not enough. It tells Him that He messed up on His plans for our life and that our plans are better. This reveals a lack of love in our hearts toward God. Covetousness breaks the command to love our neighbor by revealing a resentment and jealousy that we have toward them for the life they have. Instead of being jealous, we ought to rejoice and praise God when He blesses others, just the same as when He blesses us.

What can we do to overcome this sinful attitude of the heart? One way would be to pursue a grateful heart. Scripture says to thank God in *all* circumstances (1 Thessalonians 5:18). Thus, no matter your circumstances, speak aloud a thankful prayer to God for the life and the many blessings you have. Remember that God doesn't owe you anything. He's already given you everything by sending His Son who died a horrifying death so that you could be redeemed and saved from the death you deserve.

So even if you don't feel thankful, thank God anyway. Again, part of growing in spiritual maturity is not being led by our emotions. What's remarkable about thanking God when we don't feel thankful is that the action of thanking God with your lips can sometimes affect your emotions. As John Piper says, "Your aim in loosing your tongue with words of gratitude is that God would be merciful and fill your words with the emotion of true gratitude."[5]

As believers, we need to trust in God's sovereign wisdom. If we think too much about where we "should" be or what we "should" have in life, it will hinder our spiritual growth. The enemy's trick is to ever so slightly take our eyes off of God so that we feel discouraged and discontent. These feelings steal our shalom and could potentially lead us to commit additional sins. So whatever your circumstances might be, understand that God has you there for a reason. He is teaching you, refining your character, and using you to bring glory to His name in your situation.

The Rich and Their Riches

According to James, the poor person is to rejoice because the trials of poverty provide opportunities to grow in wisdom and faith. Likewise, the rich person is to rejoice in his humiliation (vv. 9-10). That is to say, when a rich person is humbled by trials, they are reminded of what truly matters in life from an eternal perspective. As James says, worldly riches and status will someday pass away. Our Messiah Yeshua taught the same thing:

---

5 John Piper, *When I Don't Desire God: How to Fight for Joy* (Wheaton, IL: Crossway, 2013), p. 222

> Do not lay up for yourselves treasures on earth, where moth and rust destroy and where thieves break in and steal, but lay up for yourselves treasures in heaven, where neither moth nor rust destroys and where thieves do not break in and steal. For where your treasure is, there your heart will be also. (Matthew 6:19-21)

Yeshua taught us not to focus so much on our worldly wealth and status. All of that stuff won't last. The moths and rust will take it from us in the end. We are to focus on the treasures of heaven—that is, the things that last for eternity. The wisdom God gives us enables us to see wealth from His perspective so that we will get our priorities straitened out. This life is not about health, wealth, and prosperity—trials remind us of that.

Now, wealth is not inherently evil. The Bible never says that it is. It's the *idolatry* of wealth that is sinful and destructive. Or as Paul puts it, "The *love of* money is a root of all kinds of evils" (1 Timothy 6:10, emphasis added). So the question is not whether wealth is bad. The question is this: What are you doing with your wealth? Where does it go? Because where you put your wealth is where your heart is. And if you are not putting your wealth into the things of God, your heart is not God's.

In light of this biblical view of wealth, Paul has some additional instruction for rich brothers and sisters:

> As for the rich in this present age, charge them not to be haughty, nor to set their hopes on the uncertainty of riches, but on God, who richly provides us with everything to enjoy. They are to do good, to be rich in good works, to be generous and ready to share, thus storing up treasure for themselves as a

> good foundation for the future, so that they may take hold of that which is truly life. (1 Timothy 6:17-19)

If God has blessed you with wealth, do not "set your hopes on the uncertainty of riches." As both James and Yeshua say, from an eternal perspective, worldly wealth will wither away. Your wealth doesn't determine your value from God's perspective. Your devotion to God and your generosity and care for the poor and those in need are the treasures of heaven. Make sure your identity and purpose in life is not in the things that pass away, but in the things that have eternal worth. Your focus on the treasures of heaven is the key to taking hold of "that which is truly life."

CHAPTER 4

RESIST TEMPTATION

Let no one say when he is tempted, "I am being tempted by God," for God cannot be tempted with evil, and he himself tempts no one. But each person is tempted when he is lured and enticed by his own desire. Then desire when it has conceived gives birth to sin, and sin when it is fully grown brings forth death.

James 1:13-15

James addresses a possible false conclusion that some people might come to when they are in the midst of trials: "I am being tempted by God!" James rejects the validity of such an idea: "God cannot be tempted with evil, and he himself tempts no one" (v. 13). In other words, temptation to sin or do evil does not come from God—it cannot. According to James, sin originates from our own hearts. Yeshua taught the same thing: "For from within, out of the heart of man, come evil thoughts, sexual immorality, theft, murder, adultery, coveting, wickedness, deceit, sensuality, envy, slander, pride, foolishness" (Mark 7:21-22). Paul wrote about the struggle between living a holy life for God and the desire to continue in sin as a "war" between his mind, which serves the law of God, and his flesh—that is, his carnal nature—which serves the law of sin (Romans 7:7-25).

While we're often inclined to blame others—including God (e.g. Proverbs 19:3)—for our difficulties, the consequences we experience from giving into temptation to sin are nobody's fault but our own. Like bait to a fish, our own desire lures us to bite down on the hook, bringing forth death. Thus, since temptation originates from our own hearts, James says that we must take responsibility for ourselves and "receive with meekness the implanted word" (James 1:21) through the work of the Holy Spirit, which will empower us to overcome sin.

The Blame Game

We are naturally inclined to blame someone or something else for our problems. For selfish reasons, we don't like to take responsibility for our mistakes. We don't like to deal with the consequences. It shouldn't surprise us to discover that we've been this way since the beginning. Here is how the first humans reacted when God confronted them about their sin:

> The man said, "The woman whom you gave to be with me, she gave me fruit of the tree, and I ate." Then the Lord God said to the woman, "What is this that you have done?" The woman said, "The serpent deceived me, and I ate." (Genesis 3:12-13)

When the Lord questioned Adam about eating the forbidden fruit, what did Adam do? Instead of owning his mistake and seeking forgiveness, he immediately blamed Eve. Then, when the Lord questioned Eve, rather than taking responsibility for her decision, she blamed the serpent. Indeed, blame-shifting is the oldest human reaction to our own sin. Since the fall, every generation of humans has sought to escape responsibility by blaming others.

You might say, "I never blame other people for my problems!" Perhaps that's true. Maybe you know better than to blame another person for your mistakes. But too often we still try to find a way to place the blame elsewhere—like on our circumstances. This is called making excuses for ourselves: "Well, I wouldn't have done that if such-and-such didn't happen!" This, too, is playing the blame game. Whatever happens in your life, it is ultimately your responsibility how you handle it. If you get arrested for robbing a bank, you won't be able to get out of jail by trying to explain to the cops that you lost your job the week before. Regardless of your circumstances, your choices are *your* choices. And if you react poorly in a situation, you have no one and nothing to blame but yourself.

Winning the War Within

Disciples of Yeshua are called to stop living in sin (Romans 6:1-2). We are called to resist temptation and pursue righteousness according to God's ways. This is the only way to truly have life and blessing. Living in sin ultimately brings about only sorrow and death. This is the consistent message throughout the Bible from the very beginning:

> But of the tree of the knowledge of good and evil you shall not eat, for in the day that you eat of it *you shall surely die.* (Genesis 2:17, emphasis added)

When Adam and Eve broke God's command and ate from the tree, they sinned. As a result, they were exiled from the presence of God and given over to death. But Adam and Eve aren't the only ones who have eaten from the tree. We all have. The Bible says that *all* have sinned (Romans 3:23). Every time we transgress God's holy and perfect Torah, we sin (Romans 3:30; 7:7; 1 John 3:4). Every time we engage in sexual activity outside of the boundaries of marriage, or cheat somebody, or lash out in anger toward our neighbor, we take a bite of that forbidden fruit just like Adam and Eve did.

This is the struggle of believers. We desire to live a life of obedience to God, but we seem to be in a constant battle against the desire of our fleshly nature to give into temptation. As Paul puts it, our mind, which serves the law of God, is at "war" with our flesh, which serves the law of sin (Romans 7:25). And all too often it seems that we lose this war. In moments of temptation, when we are "lured and enticed" by our own desire (v. 14), it's so easy to focus only on the temporary gratification of giving into sin that we forget the pain, sorrow, and death that come with it. We are just like the Israelites who, after they were miraculously delivered from slavery, longed to return to Egypt. They longed for the delicious food that they ate in Egypt (Numbers 11:5), forgetting all about the life of slavery they were made to endure. This is why Paul reminds us of the end result of sin:

> But what fruit were you getting at that time from the things of which you are now ashamed? For the end of those things is death. (Romans 6:21)

Sin is grievous and destructive. Engaging in it hurts not only us but also others. It brings nothing but shame and death. Worst of all, sin distorts the image of God that we are called to bear. If we are going to be effective in fulfilling our purpose as a light to the nations, then overcoming sin is imperative. So how do we say "no" to temptation and break free from the sin in our lives?

Before we answer that question, we need to understand that we cannot be perfectly sinless on this side of eternity. John said, "If we say we have no sin, we deceive ourselves, and the truth is not in us" (1 John 1:8). Indeed, because of the weakness of our flesh, believers will still give in to sin from time to time. However, while we will never be perfect until we are given immortal bodies at the resurrection, the Bible gives us answers on how we can gradually and increasingly overcome sin in this life.

The first step to overcoming sin is to understand that while we do sin, we have an advocate with the Father—Yeshua our Messiah (1 John

2:1). If we confess our sins to God, He is faithful to forgive us and cleanse us from all unrighteousness (1 John 1:9). So overcoming sin begins with opening your heart and truly receiving God's forgiveness. After Paul describes this war between the desire to obey God and the desire to sin that is raging within us, he teaches us how to win this war. And he begins his answer with a reminder that those who know Messiah Yeshua are not condemned (Romans 8:1). This first step is important because few things hinder us from having victory over sin more than self-condemnation. The enemy of our souls, Satan, loves to hold our past over our heads. But what good does feeling condemned do? Does it glorify God to emotionally punish ourselves rather than fall into God's loving embrace? Not at all. Self-condemnation is unproductive and actually keeps people from repentance.

Now conviction is not the same as self-condemnation. We should, of course, feel guilty and convicted when we fall short. If we truly love God, how could we not feel terrible about being unfaithful to Him? But conviction has a goal. God uses our conviction to move us to repentance so that our fellowship with Him can be renewed and so we can get back on the right path. Satan, on the other hand, exploits our guilt in order to bind us deeper into self-condemnation, rendering us useless to the kingdom of God. Satan wants us to dwell on our shortcomings and believe we are unable to change and should just give up rather than receive God's grace and keep moving forward in faith. But we must not give up. Imagine if Abraham, Moses, or King David gave up the times they fell short! Scripture commands us, "As the Lord has forgiven you, so you also must forgive" (Colossians 3:13). Sometimes the person we need to forgive is ourselves.

The second step to overcoming sin is to walk according to the Spirit. Paul taught that when we walk according to the Spirit, the righteous requirement of the Torah is fulfilled in us (Romans 8:3-4) and we will not gratify the desires of our flesh (Galatians 5:16-17). The Holy Spirit writes God's Torah on our hearts (Jeremiah 31:33) and thus creates within us the desire to obey God. When we have this desire on our heart, keeping the Torah is no longer a burden but a blessing. Moreover, when we sin by transgressing the Torah, we grieve the Holy Spirit within us. But our obedience to God's ways pleases the Holy Spirit. As we walk according to the Spirit throughout our Christian lives, the desire to obey God becomes stronger to the point where it outweighs the desire to do evil.

It should be understood that walking according to the Spirit means not only avoiding what's contrary to God's will but also immersing yourself in the things of God. Like we see in any relationship, a healthy and lasting bond requires you to be intentional. So it is with our relationship with the Lord. The more we immerse ourselves in the things of God—studying His Word, spending time in prayer, getting involved with our local congregation—the more we grow in our desire to be obedient and say no to sin. On the other hand, the more time and energy we invest in the world—binge-watching trashy TV shows on Netflix, engaging in gossip and evil speech with others, mindlessly scrolling our social media feeds—the more our desire for the world grows. This old poem from an anonymous author puts it well:

> Two natures beat within my breast
> The one is foul, the one is blessed
> The one I love, the other I hate
> The one I feed will dominate[1]

---

1 Cited in Tara Leigh Cobble, *Crowded Skies: Letters to Manhattan* (Shrinking Music Publishing, 2007), p. 1

The third step to overcoming sin is to set up boundaries. That is to say, as much as possible, don't allow yourself to be in the position where you could give in to temptation to sin. This applies especially to sexual sin. The Apostle Paul tells us to "flee from sexual immorality" (1 Corinthians 6:18) for a reason. He doesn't tell us to stand firm and resist—he says to run away! We can look to Joseph as an example of this. When Potiphar's wife tried to seduce Joseph, what did he do? He didn't just stand there—he immediately fled the house to get away from her (Genesis 39:12).

In a world where 64% of Christian men and 15% of Christian women admit to watching porn at least once a month,[2] it's safe to conclude that most believers are not strong enough to resist the temptation to engage in sexual sin such as pornography. And our culture and technology doesn't make it any easier for us. This quote from the U.S. Department of Justice is quite alarming:

> Never before in the history of telecommunications media in the United States has so much indecent (and obscene) material been so easily accessible by so many minors in so many American homes with so few restrictions.[3]

Technology and our culture will not restrict us from accessing sinful material online. Therefore, we must set up boundaries to restrict ourselves. We ought to follow Joseph's lead. Don't stay in the room with Potiphar's wife—not even for a second. Immediately get off the

---

2 CovenantEyes, *Pornography Statistics: 250+ facts, quotes, and statistics about pornography use* (2015 Edition), p. 20

3 Ibid., p. 13

Internet, turn off your computer, and go outside. Don't even give yourself the chance to give in to sexual sin.

The fourth step is to ask God to help you see sin the way He does. Ask Him to help you hate your sin the way He hates it. Ask Him to help you grasp in your heart the price that was paid so that you could be redeemed. As Charles Spurgeon once said, "Sin has been pardoned at such a price that we cannot henceforth trifle with it."[4] As blood-bought sons and daughters of the Most High God, may we pursue holiness and purity. May we truly grasp the great price our Savior paid for our redemption that we may be given the strength to turn from sin and live for Him.

---

4 Charles Spurgeon, *The Complete Works of C. H. Spurgeon, Vol. 32: Sermons 1877-1937* (Delmarva Publications, Inc.) p. 684

CHAPTER 5

TRUST IN GOD'S GOODNESS

Do not be deceived, my beloved brothers. Every good gift and every perfect gift is from above, coming down from the Father of lights, with whom there is no variation or shadow due to change. Of his own will he brought us forth by the word of truth, that we should be a kind of firstfruits of his creatures.
James 1:16-18

In the prior passage, James taught us that the end result of sin is death. In this passage, he teaches us that the end result of being brought forth "by the word of truth" is new birth and identity. Life, purpose, maturity, wisdom—these are among the good gifts that God gives us. Here James sets up a dichotomy between our own (selfish) desires that he addressed in the previous passage, which bring forth death and disorder, and the wisdom and purpose we receive from God, which brings forth life and peace. James will expound on this dichotomy throughout the rest of his epistle.

When we are faced with trials, we might be tempted to doubt the goodness of God. That's why James says, "Do not be deceived" (v. 16). He then reminds us that every good thing we have is from God. In addition to doubting God's goodness, some suffering believers might be tempted to think that God is capricious and unreliable. But James explains that there's "no variation or shadow" with God (v. 17). That is to say, He doesn't change (e.g. Malachi 3:6). He is faithful, He cares, and He will always give good gifts to His children. In light of God's sovereignty and care for His children, He is called the Father of lights, which, according to Keener, could mean "Creator of the stars":

> Many people believed that stars controlled their fate in arbitrary ways, but James instead proclaims that our lives rest in the hands of a loving Father.[1]

Among God's good gifts to us is a new identity and purpose in His plan as a "firstfruits of his creatures." Just as the firstfruits are offered to the Lord in anticipation of the full harvest to follow, we as the firstfruits of God's creatures represent the hope of the ingathering of the nations. It's through us as adopted children of Abraham in the Messiah that "all the families of the earth shall be blessed" (Genesis 12:3). That's our mission as Yeshua's disciples—to glorify God and be a light to the nations. James encourages us to trust in God's goodness, resist the temptation to sin, and fulfill our purpose even in the midst of trials and persecution.

Reviving Your Hope in God

The difficulties that we endure in this life are sometimes so painful that it's easy to forget about God's goodness. Many people go through tragedies that leave them with a crushing despair, which years later turns into a continuous dull ache that never leaves. They become despondent and therefore reluctant to believe that God could heal them or that He even cares.

These deep, painful emotions are not foreign to the Bible. For instance, when the Israelites were in Egypt, they were so utterly overwhelmed by the oppression they faced that when Moses finally came to tell them of God's promise to deliver them, they simply couldn't believe him:

---

1 Craig Keener, *NIV Cultural Backgrounds Study Bible: Bringing to Life the Ancient World of Scripture*, James 1:17 (Grand Rapids, MI: Zondervan, 2016)

> Moses spoke thus to the people of Israel, but they did not listen to Moses, because of their broken spirit and harsh slavery. (Exodus 6:9).

Of course, we know the story. God was faithful to deliver them according to His Word. He doesn't change His mind or forget. He doesn't make empty promises or fail to follow through with what He said He would do. As Scripture declares, "God is not a man, that he should lie, or a son of man, that he should change his mind" (Numbers 23:19).

With that in mind, hasn't God likewise promised to deliver us? Scripture says, in the world to come (otherwise known as eternal life), God will wipe away every tear from our eyes and there will be no more pain or death (Revelation 21:4), and we'll receive a crown of life for our faithfulness (James 1:12). In the meantime, if we remain steadfast in the midst of trials, we're told that our faith will be strengthened and we'll become spiritually mature (James 1:2-4). God is involved every step of the way, and He knows what He's doing.

While difficult circumstances might make it hard to trust in God's wisdom and goodness, we are to walk by faith, not by sight (2 Corinthians 5:7). But that's easier said than done, isn't it? Even as we have these great assurances of God's love and good purpose in the midst of our suffering, like the Israelites in Egypt, it's still hard to hope sometimes. And thus, there is no relief from our pain. So what do we do? How do we revive our hope?

Unlike what we hear in some religious circles—usually those that tend to emphasize "health, wealth, and prosperity"—the first step to revived hope is to understand that it's okay to be honest about how we feel. It's normal to be sad and troubled in the midst of trials. It's okay that the pain from loss and suffering and betrayal might linger in our hearts. Moreover, it's okay to express our pain and doubts to God. Israel has a rich tradition of lament. Consider Jeremiah who cried out, "Why did I come out from the womb to see toil and sorrow, and spend my days in shame?" (Jeremiah 20:18) All throughout the Bible are examples of people crying out to God, weeping and passionately airing their hurts. An entire book of the Bible—Lamentations—is devoted to a lament over the destruction of Jerusalem. Indeed, to shun the bitter expression of grief and sorrow, as some religious circles do, is neither human nor biblical.

The second step to revived hope, as we covered in chapter 1, is to understand that God has a special place in His heart for hurting people. We can take comfort in the fact that He is near to the brokenhearted (Psalm 34:18). As Christian Holocaust survivor Corrie Ten Boom wrote, "There is no pit so deep that He is not deeper still."[2] In the depths of our despair, we can experience God's divine presence in a profound way. He is near to us, weeping as we weep (John 11:33-36), and carrying us through the pain.

The third step to revived hope is to remember and reflect on what God has done in your life. Despite everything you might be going through right now, God sent His Son to die so that you could be delivered from sin and death. He has given you a new life of purpose. When we remember all that God has done for us, it often rekindles a fire in our hearts for the Lord. This is one of the reasons the Bible gives us so many memorials commemorating God's work in the lives of His people. For instance, every Sabbath we're commanded to remember our deliverance from Egypt (Deuteronomy 5:15), which is a direct prophecy of our salvation in Messiah. Just as God delivered Israel

---

2 Corrie Ten Boom, *The Hiding Place: 35th Anniversary Edition* (Grand Rapids, MI: Chosen Books of Baker Publishing Group, 2006).

from slavery in Egypt, Yeshua's work on the cross has rescued us from the slavery of our sins. Thus, every Sabbath we reflect on the Gospel message. The Bible also emphasizes the need for believers to regularly attend church and fellowship with other believers. When we worship God, sing praises to Him, and hear testimonies of His mighty works, we are reminded of His goodness.

The third step is to wait. As it is written in Psalms:

> *I waited patiently* for the Lord; he inclined to me and heard my cry. He drew me up from the pit of destruction, out of the miry bog, and set my feet upon a rock, making my steps secure. He put a new song in my mouth, a song of praise to our God. Many will see and fear, and put their trust in the Lord. (Psalm 40:1-3, emphasis added)

We don't know how long the psalmist had to wait before God pulled him out of the pit of destruction and put a new song of praise in his mouth, but it most likely took much longer than he would have liked. There's a lot of truth to the saying, "Time heals all wounds." Some spiritual and emotional wounds simply require time in order to heal. Many believers have waited for years before finally getting breakthrough, all the while staying faithful to God in the midst of the pain.

The fourth step is to serve others. As it is written in Isaiah:

> If you pour yourself out for the hungry and satisfy the desire of the afflicted, then shall your light rise in the darkness and your gloom be as the noonday. (Isaiah 58:10)

When we focus on ministering to other people, God somehow uses it to minister to us. It helps us to not be so absorbed in our own misery and realize that we have a role in bringing life and healing to a hurting world. The pain we endure is actually in a way redeemed when we allow God to use us to help others through their pain. That is, if we had not gone through some of the things we've gone through, we would not be able to bring hope and healing to those who have similar painful experiences.

If you're struggling to believe in God's goodness because of trials, perhaps following these steps will help you get a taste of the complete healing that awaits you when Messiah Yeshua returns and ushers in His Kingdom in which pain and death are abolished. May your hope in God be revived as you embrace His divine presence in the midst of your sorrow. May you be encouraged as you see His hand move in your ministry to other hurting people.

CHAPTER 6

CONTROL YOUR EMOTIONS

Know this, my beloved brothers: let every person be quick to hear, slow to speak, slow to anger; for the anger of man does not produce the righteousness of God. Therefore put away all filthiness and rampant wickedness and receive with meekness the implanted word, which is able to save your souls.

James 1:19-21

James begins this next passage with an admonition to not immediately react out of anger but to be patient, loving, and kind. Why? Because reacting out of anger and vindictive emotion does not bring forth righteousness but breeds sin, chaos, and destruction. A few verses later, he says that if you think you're religious but can't control your speech, then your religion is "worthless" (James 1:26). James' admonition against anger here echoes what Yeshua taught in His Sermon on the Mount:

> You have heard that it was said to those of old, 'You shall not murder; and whoever murders will be liable to judgment.' But I say to you that everyone who is angry with his brother will be liable to judgment; whoever insults his brother will be liable to the council; and whoever says, 'You fool!' will be liable to the hell of fire. (Matthew 5:21-22)

Scholars believe that Yeshua's words here are construed in a three-tiered progression.[1] That is to say, anger, when left unchecked, leads to insults, and insults lead to slander ("you fool"). As each offense increases in severity, the offender is liable to increasingly powerful courts—all the way to "the hell of fire." Tim Hegg observes:

> Yeshua is showing the progression of anger, which begins inwardly but if allowed to remain to grow, evidences outward, destructive behavior. Indeed, this is why it is linked with murder. In Gen 4:5 we learn that Cain became "very angry," which eventually led to the crime of murder against his brother. Thus, what might be considered a light commandment, "You shall not hate your fellow man (literally "your brother") in your heart" (Lev 19:17) must be rather understood as a weighty one, because left to grow, the possibility is ripe that it will proceed to a whole garden of sins, including murder.[2]

James articulates this same idea. Earlier in his epistle, he already taught about how sin begins inwardly when one is "lured and enticed by his own desire" (James 1:14). When we do not deal with the evil inclinations of our hearts, the inevitable result is outward sin such as violence. (This message was especially relevant to James' original audience who was suffering tremendous oppression at the hands of the Romans and the rich aristocracy, leading many to want to revolt.)[3] So what is the answer to truly overcoming sin? How do we

---

1 Tim Hegg, *Commentary on the Gospel of Matthew Chapters 1-7* (Tacoma, WA: TorahResource, 2007) p. 195

2 Ibid., pp. 195-196

3 Craig Keener, *NIV Cultural Backgrounds Study Bible: Bringing to Life the Ancient World of Scripture*, James 1:20 (Grand Rapids, MI: Zondervan, 2016)

gain control over our emotions and speech? We begin with the heart. Yeshua said "what comes out of the mouth proceeds from the heart" (Matthew 15:18). That is why James says, "Receive with meekness the implanted word, which is able to save your souls" (v. 21). In order to walk in the righteousness that God requires of us, the Torah—the word of God—must be written on our hearts. As J.K. McKee remarks:

> The presence of "the implanted word" has been most appropriately compared to the salvific power of the prophesied New Covenant in the Tanach (Jeremiah 31:31-34; Ezekiel 36:25-27), by various commentators. Not only would this involve a permanent forgiveness and cleansing from sins, but the implantation of a new heart, *and* the supernatural compulsion to obey the Lord's commandments by His Spirit.[4]

Just as Yeshua taught in His parable of the sower (Matthew 13:18-23), only when we receive the word and understand it—that is, allow it to be planted in the "good soil" of our hearts—will we bear fruit. That fruit is a transformed life in the Messiah, a heartfelt obedience to the Torah out of love for God and our neighbor, and godly character and wisdom (James 3:17; Galatians 5:22-23). These things are the evidence of our salvation.

Self-Control in the Midst of Conflict

Can you recall times in your life when you've lost control of your emotions? Perhaps it happens more often than you'd like to admit.

---

4 J.K. McKee, *James for the Practical Messianic* (Richardson, TX: Messianic Apologetics, 2013), pp. 41-42

We've all had heated moments where we've reacted out of anger or pain, often provoking others and dragging out arguments. What guidance do the Scriptures give us in these situations?

In the book of Genesis, we read about Jacob's son, Joseph. Joseph was a passionate young man who was given amazing dreams by God. In his excitement and immaturity, he shared these dreams with his brothers who were already annoyed with and jealous of Joseph because he was their father's favorite son. Their hatred of Joseph eventually reached the point where they decided to get rid of him. They pushed him down a pit, sold him into slavery, and convinced their father that he had been killed by a wild animal. Joseph was taken to Egypt where he was later falsely accused of attempted rape and thrown into prison.

While Joseph faced many trials and tribulations—betrayal, loss, being lied about, etc.—God used those difficult situations to bring Joseph to the place where he could be used to accomplish God's will. Through a series of miraculous events in prison, Joseph was given the opportunity to directly connect with the Pharaoh. And through that contact, Joseph was given authority over all of Egypt. While God orchestrated these events to bring Joseph to this place, these events also served to help Joseph grow in maturity and wisdom.

After several years, a famine had spread over all the land—and once again, God orchestrated this event for His purposes. This famine caused Jacob to send Joseph's brothers to buy grain from Egypt, and there they encountered Joseph. But, after so many years, they didn't recognize him. Not yet revealing his true identity to his brothers, Joseph ordered them to bring Benjamin—Joseph's full brother, the only other son of his mother Rachel—to Egypt. When they arrived again with Benjamin, we see that Joseph became utterly overwhelmed with emotion:

> And he lifted up his eyes and saw his brother Benjamin, his mother's son, and said, "Is this your youngest brother, of whom you spoke to me? God be gracious to you, my son!" Then Joseph hurried out, for his compassion grew warm for his brother, and he sought a place to weep. And he entered his chamber and wept there. Then he washed his face and came out. *And controlling himself* he said, "Serve the food." (Genesis 43:29-31, emphasis added)

Can you imagine the flood of emotions Joseph must have felt in that moment? Reconnecting with his family likely brought about immense joy mixed with anger and the ache of betrayal. He was glad to see them, but he most likely still dealt with painful memories of being hated and abandoned. The trials that Joseph faced caused him to grow in spiritual maturity and wisdom, but painful feelings can still linger with us for many years no matter how mature we are. Noticing that he was overwhelmed, and not wanting to ruin this chance to reconcile with his family, Joseph excused himself so that he could find "a place to weep." He didn't ignore or suppress his emotions as if they didn't matter. He simply chose not to be mastered by them. After removing himself from the situation until he could regain control of his emotions, Joseph was able to return to the company of his brothers without causing any drama.

We've all been in sensitive situations where emotions ran high. The lesson here is not that we should bottle our feelings, which certainly wouldn't be healthy or biblical, but that we ought to ask God to help us recognize when we're about to be pushed beyond what we can handle. And in those heated moments, when we feel like we are about to jump off the edge, we are to choose self-control, a fruit of the Spirit (Galatians 5:23). A practical way we can do that is to do what Joseph did—that is, step away from the situation for a short time. After we vent, weep, pray, or do whatever we have to do in private to regain control, we can then return to resolve the conflict peacefully.

As we continue with Joseph's story, despite the stinging pain of betrayal, we see that he was able to see the bigger purpose in his suffering. This was key to his ability to truly forgive and reconcile with his family. Even though he had the opportunity to get revenge, he was able to move forward in love and kindness:

> But Joseph said to them, "Do not fear, for am I in the place of God? As for you, you meant evil against me, but God meant it for good, to bring it about that many people should be kept alive, as they are today. So do not fear; I will provide for you and your little ones." Thus he comforted them and spoke kindly to them. (Genesis 50:19-21)

Next time you find yourself in a heated argument or some other conflict, as you recognize that you're about to lose control, step away. Go into another room. Take a deep breath. Try to see the bigger purpose in what you're going through and how God might be using the situation for His glory and your spiritual benefit. Then come back when you aren't overwhelmed by emotion and can address the situation with wisdom and shalom as a disciple of Yeshua.

Do What's Right (Even When You Don't Want To)

Emotions are powerful. Our emotions, like compassion and empathy, often motivate us to do wonderful things like give to charity and help people in need. When we see an injustice, many times it will deeply affect us and move us to take positive action. And yet, on the other hand, strong negative emotions—jealousy, vindictiveness, resentment—can often overpower our better judgment and move us to neglect or hurt people. Indeed, our sinful inclination influences our emotions and therefore our behavior. Thus, we oftentimes must ignore our feelings in order to do what's right.

The Torah takes direct aim at how our negative emotions might affect us:

> If you meet your enemy's ox or his donkey going astray, you shall bring it back to him. If you see the donkey of one who hates you lying down under its burden, you shall refrain from leaving him with it; you shall rescue it with him. (Exodus 23:4-5)

Here we see that we are commanded, in some circumstances, to ignore our emotions. When you see that your enemy—that is, someone who "hates you"—is in need, you are to go out of your way to help them regardless of your feelings or theirs. While you would naturally feel angry or vindictive toward that person and want to therefore ignore their need, you must set those feelings aside.

These commandments follow directly after a passage that concerns upholding justice in court (Exodus 23:1-3). This principle applies here as well. For instance, while we might feel inclined to side with the majority because we feel more comfortable just sticking with the crowd, we are not to pervert justice. Also, while we might feel bad about a poor person's circumstances, we are explicitly commanded not to slant our testimony in favor of them in their lawsuit. Our sole concern must be what is true and fair. If justice isn't about truth and fairness, it simply isn't real justice. And if there is no justice, society breaks down.

Again, emotions are powerful. And negative emotions toward our enemies have an impact on our behavior, which has an impact on society as a whole. As disciples of Yeshua, we are called to the standard of Scripture. We are commissioned to uphold righteousness and justice and make a positive impact in our communities for God's glory. That's why Yeshua expounds on these Torah principles in His Sermon on the Mount:

> You have heard that it was said, "You shall love your neighbor and hate your enemy. But I say to you, Love your enemies and pray for those who persecute you, so that you may be sons of your Father who is in heaven. For he makes his sun rise on the evil and on the good, and sends rain on the just and on the unjust. For if you love those who love you, what reward do you have? Do not even the tax collectors do the same? And if you greet only your brothers, what more are you doing than others? Do not even the Gentiles do the same? You therefore must be perfect, as your heavenly Father is perfect." (Matthew 5:43-48)

Yeshua calls us to love our enemies. But how can we possibly do that? Isn't love connected to our emotions? And while we might be able to ignore our emotions, we certainly can't change them, right? While it's true that love has emotional aspects, in the Bible love is often connected to what we do. Like our passage from the Torah, Yeshua gives us practical steps on loving our enemy. What's profound is that following these practical steps can also have an effect on our emotions.

According to Yeshua, the first step to loving our enemies is to pray for them. God is moved by our prayers not only for the sake of our enemy but also for the sake of our own hearts. When we sincerely pray for the people who hate us and who have hurt us, God changes the way we see them. He helps us to stop dehumanizing them and seeing them only as the person who caused us pain. God helps us see them as our neighbor—a flawed but generally good-intentioned person like us—rather than our enemy. Prayer is powerful and transformative. As the actor who played C.S. Lewis in the 1993 movie *Shadowlands* so eloquently put it:

> I pray because I can't help myself. I pray because I'm helpless. I pray because the need flows out of me all the time, waking and sleeping. It doesn't change God. It changes me.[5]

The second step is to meet their needs. Just as God causes the sun to shine and the rain to fall on His enemies, we ought to look for opportunities to meet the needs of our enemies. This goes right back to our passage from Exodus. Regardless of our emotions toward the person who hates us, we must do the right thing.

Third, Yeshua says that we are to greet our enemies. Setting aside grudges and bitterness to muster up a friendly "hello" goes a long way. And again, following these practical steps can potentially impact our own feelings. Who knows? Simply greeting your enemy could perhaps open the door to eventually restoring a friendship. We should never think that a broken relationship is beyond God's ability to repair. Philosopher Søren Kierkegaard put it well:

> Never cease loving a person, and never give up hope for him, for even the prodigal son who had fallen most low, could still be saved; the bitterest enemy and also he who was your

---

5 *Shadowlands*. "Quotes." www.imdb.com. Accessed 10/7/18

> friend could again be your friend; love that has grown cold can kindle.[6]

While it's good to hope for such things, the bottom line is still that we are to do the right thing simply because it's the right thing. God has not called us to be led by our emotions but by His Spirit. We can hope that God changes hearts (especially our own). We can hope that God restores relationships and turns enemies into friends again. But in the meantime, regardless of how we feel, we set our emotions aside to do what's right.

Listen When A Donkey Speaks

Feelings are important and shouldn't be dismissed. But we must not be led by our feelings. We cannot assume that our feelings reflect the complete truth of any situation. Our feelings reflect only *how we interpret* the truth of the situation. New information or another perspective often leads to a different interpretation.

Consider the story of Balaam's donkey. One day Balaam was riding his donkey, but the donkey kept turning from the path and eventually crushed Balaam's foot against a wall. Balaam's immediate emotional reaction was to beat his donkey. Why? Because Balaam felt like his donkey was just trying to make him feel foolish:

> Then the Lord opened the mouth of the donkey, and she said to Balaam, "What have I done to you, that you have struck me these three times?" And Balaam said to the donkey, "Because

---

6 Referenced in: Martin H. Manser, *The Westminster Collection of Christian Quotations* (Louisville, KY: Westminster John Knox Press, 2001) p. 177

> you have made a fool of me. I wish I had a sword in my hand, for then I would kill you." (Numbers 22:28-29)

Balaam felt foolish and reacted to this situation by beating and cursing his donkey. But his donkey wasn't trying to make Balaam feel foolish. In reality, the donkey was saving Balaam's life because the Angel of the Lord was going to kill him:

> And the angel of the Lord said to him, "Why have you struck your donkey these three times? Behold, I have come out to oppose you because your way is perverse before me. The donkey saw me and turned aside before me these three times. If she had not turned aside from me, surely just now I would have killed you and let her live." (Numbers 22:32-33)

Based on the information Balaam had before he noticed the Angel of the Lord, his feelings were understandable. However, his actions—beating his donkey—were not a good example of how we should handle our feelings. After all, Balaam knew his donkey his entire life (Numbers 22:30). He should have known better to at least stop, take a deep breath, and look around before immediately reacting out of hurt and anger. Balaam eventually found out what was actually going on, which helped to address his feelings about his donkey's behavior—but it was only after he had reacted in a hurtful way.

How often have you reacted from your hurt feelings, which led you to do or say something you later regretted? Like Balaam, how often have you lashed out at people who were simply trying to warn you about going down a destructive path? How often have you cursed those who care about you and severed relationships because people offended you?

Again, we shouldn't dismiss our feelings. But the fruit of the Spirit includes self-control. Unlike Balaam, we must not immediately assume that we have all the facts or that we know someone's true motives. We must avoid reacting to a situation emotionally by saying or doing something hurtful. We must lead our feelings rather than letting our feelings lead us.

In addition to not reacting in a hurtful way, we should consider that our friends who are willing to offend us are trying to help us out of love and concern. King David said, "Let a righteous man strike me—it is a kindness; let him rebuke me—it is oil for my head; let my head not refuse it" (Psalm 141:5). A true friend is willing to rebuke you. You might think they're being a complete jerk in the moment, but sometimes God speaks through a "donkey." Be humble. Instead of getting offended and lashing out, maybe try listening to what they have to say. It just might save your life.

CHAPTER 7

PRACTICE PURE RELIGION

But be doers of the word, and not hearers only, deceiving yourselves. For if anyone is a hearer of the word and not a doer, he is like a man who looks intently at his natural face in a mirror. For he looks at himself and goes away and at once forgets what he was like. But the one who looks into the perfect law, the law of liberty, and perseveres, being no hearer who forgets but a doer who acts, he will be blessed in his doing. If anyone thinks he is religious and does not bridle his tongue but deceives his heart, this person's religion is worthless. Religion that is pure and undefiled before God the Father is this: to visit orphans and widows in their affliction, and to keep oneself unstained from the world.

James 1:22-27

In the previous passage, James spoke of the need for believers to "receive with meekness the implanted word." Now he brings that idea to its conclusion—believers are to be "doers of the word, and not hearers only." True and saving faith is made evident by our behavior. James will develop this further throughout his epistle and especially at the end of chapter two. This, of course, echoes the teachings of Yeshua, who said, "Blessed rather are those who hear the word of God and keep it" (Luke 11:28).

Doing the word entails Torah observance. As scholar and theologian Scot McKnight observes, "Torah and 'do' (*'asah*) are brought together so often in the Hebrew Bible that instinct ought to lead us to see here a form of Torah observance."[1] Likewise, J.K. McKee remarks that James 1:22 "is one of the most forthright words in favor of Torah

---

1 Scot McKnight, *The New International Commentary of the New Testament: The Letter of James* (Grand Rapids, MI: Wm. B. Eerdmans Publishing Co., 2011) p. 147

observance for Messiah followers in the entire Apostolic Scriptures."[2] This fact is made all the more clear a couple verses later when James speaks of being a doer of the "perfect law, the law of liberty," which is an obvious reference to the Torah of Moses. Indeed, like Yeshua, James affirmed the ongoing validity and authority of the Torah—every "iota" and "dot" (Matthew 5:17-20). According to James, the Torah is perfect and brings liberty, echoing the attitude toward the Torah expressed in the Psalms:

> The law of the Lord is perfect, reviving the soul; the testimony of the Lord is sure, making wise the simple; the precepts of the Lord are right, rejoicing the heart; the commandment of the Lord is pure, enlightening the eyes; the feat of the Lord is clean, enduring forever; the rules of the Lord are true, and righteous altogether. More to be desired are they than gold, even much fine gold; sweeter also than honey and drippings of the honeycomb. Moreover, by them is your servant warned; in keeping them there is great reward. (Psalm 19:7-11)

Also like Yeshua, James viewed proper Torah observance as being from the basis of the New Covenant with the Torah written on the heart and summed up in love for God and our neighbor (Matthew 22:37-40; James 2:8). That is why James emphasizes holiness (keeping oneself "unstained from the world") and caring for the widows and orphans as essential to having a pure religion—that is, a proper expression of worship to God. In addition to spiritual fidelity and ministering to the marginalized, pure religion involves having self-control over our

---

2 J.K. McKee, *James for the Practical Messianic* (Richardson, TX: Messianic Apologetics, 2013), p. 43

speech. Failing to "bridle our tongue" renders our religion worthless and violates the Torah as taught by Yeshua, who said, "On the day of judgment people will give account for every careless word they speak." (Matthew 12:36).

James' use of the mirror metaphor really drives his point home. The mirror represents the Torah (v. 25), which reveals our moral responsibility to God. Once we look into the mirror, we have two options. The first option is to walk away and forget what we look like, failing to follow through with how God has called us to live. As McKnight says, "The person who hears the Word but does not do is like the person who sees *his or her own sinfulness* but does nothing about it."[3] The second option is to put our faith into action. In order to have true and lasting liberty, we must receive the implanted word on our hearts and practice pure and undefiled religion, which is summed up by James as controlling our speech, actively caring for the widows and orphans, and walking in holiness. Those who look in the mirror and persevere—that is, those who are doers of the Torah as taught and lived by Messiah Yeshua—will be blessed.

God Created You to be Free

The United States Declaration of Independence speaks of certain unalienable rights that are given to all human beings, among which are life, liberty, and the pursuit of happiness. The committee who drafted this important document didn't come up with the idea of these rights on their own. These rights, as the Declaration of Independence says, are endowed to us by the Creator. In particular, the importance of liberty is deeply grounded in the values expressed by the Bible. For

---

3 Scot McKnight, *The New International Commentary of the New Testament: The Letter of James* (Grand Rapids, MI: Wm. B. Eerdmans Publishing Co., 2011) p. 151

instance, the first of the Ten Commandments ("Ten Words" in Hebrew) deliberately reminds us of the source of true liberty:

> I am the Lord your God, who brought you out of the land of Egypt, out of the house of slavery. (Exodus 20:2)

God places a high value on liberty. The entire basis of the Torah is the declaration that we've been liberated and therefore ought to walk in liberty. In the New Testament, James calls the Torah the "law of liberty" and tells us to be doers of that word (James 1:24; 2:12). So, according to the Bible, we were not created to live as slaves, but as free people—and that means living in obedience to God's ways. As Dennis Prager so eloquently put it:

> The Giver of the Ten Commandments is, in effect, saying: "I took you out of slavery and into freedom, and these Ten Commandments are the way to make a free society. You cannot be a free people if you do whatever you want." Freedom comes from moral self-control. There is no other way to achieve it.[4]

The only time God's commandments don't bring liberty is when we break them. The Torah reveals what sin is through God's commandments (Romans 3:20). When we transgress the commandments of the Torah, we sin (Romans 7:7; 1 John 3:4). According to Scripture, we've all transgressed the Torah and thus have sinned. We've all been enslaved to our personal Egypts. But just as God delivered the Israelites from slavery in Egypt, He has delivered us from the slavery of

---

4 Dennis Prager, *Prager University*. "I am the Lord Your God." www.prageru.com. Accessed 10/9/2018

sin and death! He sent His Son, Yeshua the Messiah, to die for us and purchase our liberty. Yeshua gave His life so that we can be free.

Think about that the next time you are tempted to go back to your old sinful habits. Returning to sin is essentially putting the yoke of slavery back on your neck to see if it still fits. It's not a good look. It betrays your created purpose as a redeemed child of God. From this day forward, may you choose Yeshua. May you choose to live in obedience. May you choose liberty. As the apostle Paul said, "For freedom Christ has set us free; stand firm therefore, and do not submit again to a yoke of slavery" (Galatians 5:1)

Doing Justice

In the prophetic book of Micah, we are told what the Lord has required of His people. That is "to do justice, and to love kindness, and to walk humbly with your God" (Micah 6:8). Doing justice is a requirement of all followers of the God of Israel. But what does that mean? What is justice in the Bible, and how do we "do" it?

At the very beginning of Creation, we are told that humans were created with the special status of bearing God's image (Genesis 1:26). This implies that all humans possess intrinsic dignity and worth, which ought to be upheld and respected. It's on this basis that we can understand the biblical concept of justice.

In Hebrew, the word for justice is *mishpat*. This word has two main senses. The first deals with judging a case and rendering a proper verdict. As pastor and theologian Tim Keller explains:

> Its most basic meaning is to treat people equitably. So Leviticus 24:22 warns Israel to "have the same *mishpat* ["rule of law"] for the foreigner as the native." *Mishpat* means acquitting

> or punishing every person on the merits of the case, regardless of race or social status.[5]

As humans created in God's image, we are all equal before God. We are not to show partiality but treat everyone, regardless of who they are, with dignity and respect. *Mishpat* also refers to one's rights—that is, making sure people are given what they are due. Keller continues:

> Deuteronomy 18 directs that the priests of the tabernacle should be supported by a certain percentage of the people's income. This support is described as "the priests' *mishpat*," which means their due or their right. So we read, "Defend the rights of the poor and needy" (Proverbs 31:9). *Mishpat*, then, is giving people what they are due, whether punishment or protection or care.[6]

Biblical justice acknowledges that all humans are made in the image of God and thus have intrinsic worth. But it goes beyond that. As Micah 6:8 says, justice is an action, something we do. This "justice-ing" entails giving people their rights. Moreover, in the Bible, doing justice is most often with regard to the most vulnerable of society—the widow, orphan, sojourner, and the poor:

> "Cursed be anyone who perverts the justice due to the sojourner, the fatherless, and the widow." And all the people shall say, "Amen." (Deuteronomy 27:18)

---

5 Tim Keller, *Generous Justice: How God's Grace Makes Us Just* (New York, NY: Penguin Books, 2016), p. 3

6 Ibid., pp. 3-4

> Open your mouth for the mute, for the rights of all who are destitute. Open your mouth, judge righteously, defend the rights of the poor and needy. (Proverbs 31:8-9)

> Learn to do good; seek justice, correct oppression; bring justice to the fatherless, plead the widow's cause. (Isaiah 1:17)

Not only does justice in the Bible entail correcting injustice, but it also has the nuance of charity. God's requirement of believers to "do justice," therefore, includes giving of our time, money, and resources to meet the needs of the poor:

> Is not this the fast that I choose: to loose the bonds of wickedness, to undo the straps of the yoke, to let the oppressed go free, and to break every yoke? Is it not to share your bread with the hungry and bring the homeless poor into your house; when you see the naked, to cover him, and not to hide yourself from your own flesh? (Isaiah 58:6-7)

Doing justice is so important in the Bible that James includes it in his teaching on what it means to have an authentic expression of worship. Among other things, having a "religion that is pure and undefiled," as James puts it, entails looking after the orphans and widows in their affliction (v. 27). That is to say, followers of Yeshua have a divine mandate to do justice by taking up the care and the cause of the marginalized and oppressed. This is a major theme throughout James' epistle, and indeed, the whole Bible. The prophets in the *Tanakh* constantly connected doing justice with authentic religious expression and rebuked Israel for thinking themselves religious while neglecting the most important aspects of their religion. According to James, your religious expression is worthless if it does not prioritize justice and righteousness. This sentiment is echoed by the prophet Amos:

> I hate, I despise your feasts, and I take no delight in your solemn assemblies. Even though you offer me your burnt offerings and grain offerings, I will not accept them; and the peace offerings of your fattened animals, I will not look upon them. Take away from me the noise of your songs; to the melody of your harps I will not listen. *But let justice roll down like waters, and righteousness like an ever-flowing stream.* (Amos 5:21-24, emphasis added)

Justice and righteousness are just as important to God today as they were in the days of Amos and James. If we consider ourselves religious but do not prioritize justice and righteousness, this same rebuke applies to us. To put it in today's language, it might sound something like this: "I hate your church services! The money you placed in the offering basket means nothing to me! I do not delight in your prayers or your Bible studies. Take away from me the noise of your worship songs. Do what I require of you—minister to the single mothers, the neglected elderly, and the homeless in your community!" Are you doing justice, or is your religion worthless?

A Voice for the Voiceless

In the first chapter of Exodus, we read about two courageous Hebrew midwives, Shiphrah and Puah, who were put in a difficult situation. The king of Egypt ordered that they must kill the sons born by the Hebrew women they served. Defying this order could have cost these midwives their lives, but the Scriptures say they "feared

God and did not do as the king of Egypt commanded them, but let the male children live" (Exodus 1:15-17).

These two women, who appear for just a short time in the Scriptures, exemplify an important characteristic that God demands His people have: courage. Shiphrah and Puah are canonized in the Scriptures and will forever be remembered as the two women who defied an evil decree, saving countless lives. The Scriptures go on to state that God blessed these women for their bravery (Exodus 1:21).

Why did these women go against the command of the Pharaoh? The Bible tells us plainly that "the midwives feared God." They knew that the Pharaoh's demands were morally evil and against the character of God. Their fear of the Lord gave them the strength to stand up for life and against injustice. In the face of an evil government that was indifferent and even hostile toward the lives of these children, Shiphrah and Puah knew that it was wrong to allow those babies to die.

Today we face a similar situation. The same satanic, murderous spirit that was within the government of Egypt is still at work today, and it continues to demand the lives of innocent children. Instead of being drowned in the Nile River, today these babies are being slaughtered inside their mother's womb. While our secular culture has invented creative euphemisms to disguise the reality of what abortion is—like "women's health" and "reproductive rights"—the fact is that abortion is the murder of an innocent child.

Politicians, Hollywood, our secular culture, and even liberal "Christians" are telling us to look the other way as this is going on. But if we really have a fear of the Lord, like Shiphrah and Puah, then we should be compelled to stand up against this injustice. Yeshua said, "Truly, I say to you, as you did it to one of the least of these my brothers, you did it to me" (Matthew 25:40). Children in the womb are certainly among the "least of these." Turning our back on them is therefore turning our back on Yeshua. James says that pure religion is to care for the widow and orphan in their affliction (v. 27). The principle of the verse in James can be applied to children in the womb. As John Piper puts it, "If orphans should be cared for by God's people, how much more children whose parents reject them. And when it says, visit them 'in their distress' we may ask, Is there any place of greater distress than in the womb of a woman who gives herself over to abortion?"[7]

If you claim to fear the Lord, you cannot ignore this great evil. God requires that you have the courage to stand up against the forces of murderous evil, just as Shiphrah and Puah stood up against the murderous evil of their time. You are required to speak the truth and expose darkness. You will perhaps face criticism and be called a "bigot" by the secular culture. But don't surrender. You just might save someone's life.

---

7 John Piper, *desiringGod*. "Visiting Orphans in a World of AIDS and Abortion." www.desiringgod.org. Accessed 12/25/18

CHAPTER 8

SHOW NO PARTIALITY

My brothers, show no partiality as you hold the faith in our Lord Jesus Christ, the Lord of glory. For if a man wearing a gold ring and fine clothing comes into your assembly, and a poor man in shabby clothing also comes in, and if you pay attention to the one who wears the fine clothing and say, "You sit here in a good place," while you say to the poor man, "You stand over there," or, "Sit down at my feet," have you not then made distinctions among yourselves and become judges with evil thoughts? Listen, my beloved brothers, has not God chosen those who are poor in the world to be rich in faith and heirs of the kingdom, which he has promised to those who love him? But you have dishonored the poor man. Are not the rich the ones who oppress you, and the ones who drag you into court? Are they not the ones who blaspheme the honorable name by which you were called?

James 2:1-7

As we've seen in the first chapter of his epistle, James is intent upon calling out fakers—those who pretend to be followers of Yeshua but don't really live out their faith. James' letter is a strong rebuke against religious hypocrisy. He exposes empty "belief" and encourages us not just to believe in God but to *believe* God—and that is defined by what we do! The goal of James' epistle is to motivate his readers to be authentic followers of Yeshua who actually live in accordance to what they profess to believe. In this spirit, James moves on to a specific example of religious hypocrisy: favoring the rich and disparaging the poor.

James points out in this passage that partiality, or favoritism, is incompatible with faith in Yeshua the Messiah. After all, a major aspect of Yeshua's ministry consisted of breaking down the walls that divided mankind on the basis of race and class (Ephesians 2:11-22).

Rebuilding those walls is in direct conflict with the very work of Yeshua and the Gospel message. It's also a direct violation of the Torah, which says, "You shall not be partial to the poor or defer to the great, but in righteousness shall you judge your neighbor" (Leviticus 19:15). Insisting on rebuilding manmade divisions among ourselves, according to James, shows that we have become "judges with evil thoughts," which entails not only a corrupted mindset but also an encroachment of God's authority as the only judge: "There is only one lawgiver and judge, he who is able to save and to destroy. But who are you to judge your neighbor?" (James 4:12).

What does it mean when James says that God has "chosen those who are poor in the world to be rich in faith and heirs of the kingdom" (v. 5)? This echoes Yeshua's teaching in Luke, "Blessed are you who are poor, for yours is the kingdom of God" (Luke 6:20). Throughout the Bible, we see that God has a special concern for the poor. In the Torah, God specifically promises to hear the cries of the poor who have been neglected or mistreated (e.g. Exodus 22:27). Thus, these believers who trust in God in the midst of their poverty are "rich in faith"—they have the promise of God's special care in their difficulties and are moreover promised a "crown of life" in the world to come for their faithful endurance (James 1:12). Partiality and disregard for the poor, therefore, is directly contrary to God's character, which His people are called to emulate:

> For the Lord your God is God of gods and Lord of lords, the great, the mighty, and the awesome God, who is not partial and takes no bribe. He executes justice for the fatherless and the widow, and loves the sojourner, giving him food and clothing. (Deuteronomy 10:17-18)

Despite God's love and concern for the poor, the Messianic community to whom James writes this epistle has "dishonored the poor man" by displaying preferential treatment toward people on the basis of wealth and worldly status. This behavior not only spits in the face of Messiah, who commanded us to have compassion for the poor and said that we do to Him what we've done to the "least of these" (Matthew 25:31-45), but it's also utterly irrational. As James points out, "Are not the rich the ones who oppress you?" Indeed, some within the community are kissing up to the very same people who take advantage of them and drag them into court! Why?

Ultimately, discriminating against people on the basis of manmade distinctions such as wealth and class profanes the name of God and breaks the royal law: "You shall love your neighbor as yourself" (James 2:8). This type of behavior is completely incompatible with faith in Yeshua. All humans are made "in the likeness of God" (James 3:9)—His image—and are therefore equal before God and worthy of dignity and honor.

Yeshua the Lord of Glory

James associates Yeshua with the Greek term *doxa*, "glory," which, according to Messianic scholar J.K. McKee, is equivalent to the Hebrew *kavod*:

> Associating Yeshua with the description of *doxa*, the Septuagint equivalent of the Hebrew *kavod*, is Christologically important. *Kavod* appears in some critical Torah passages describing the Divine Presence of God [...] The term *kavod* literally means "heavy," and it has a wide variety of connotations. The most

> significant of these predominantly regards the presence of God manifested in the Tabernacle in the wilderness.[1]

The implications of James' use of the title "Lord of glory" for Yeshua are significant. While the title denotes honor, James is intending much more than honor here. Yeshua is the visible manifestation of the glory and presence of God (Hebrews 1:3). In other words, the God of Israel Himself is revealed *in* Yeshua the Messiah. This sentiment is shared by the other New Testament authors, in particular John:

> In the beginning was the Word, and the Word was with God, and the Word was God. He was in the beginning with God [...] And the Word became flesh and dwelt among us, and *we have seen His glory*, glory as of the only Son from the Father, full of truth. (John 1:1-2, 14, emphasis added)

> And now, Father, glorify me in your own presence with the glory that I had with you before the world existed. (John 17:5)

According to the apostles, Yeshua personally existed with the Father in the same divine glory before the world existed. He then "emptied Himself," took on human form, and died for our sins (Philippians 2:6-11). Now He has returned to that state of full glory and splendor at the right hand of the Father.

Another significant place where *doxa* is found is in Titus 2:13, which says that believers ought to be "waiting for our blessed hope,

1 J.K. McKee, *James for the Practical Messianic* (Richardson, TX: Messianic Apologetics, 2013), pp. 51-52

the appearing of the glory of our great God and Savior Jesus Christ." Regarding this verse, McKee remarks:

> Here, the glory in view is obviously the manifestation of God's greatness at the Second Coming—but especially not to be overlooked is how Yeshua Himself is labeled with the titles of "God and Savior," necessarily implying that the Messiah is, Himself, God.[2]

It seems clear that the apostles had no problem identifying the Messiah as "God," thus affirming His eternal divine nature. They did not see the Messiah as a mere man but as God in human flesh. In the introduction of his epistle, James describes himself as a servant of both God *and* the "Lord" (*kyrios*) Yeshua the Messiah (1:1), indicating that his allegiance to Yeshua as Lord/Master is not in conflict with his allegiance to God since they are one (John 14:10). Moreover, throughout James' epistle the title "Lord" is used in reference to the God of Israel in addition to Yeshua. In fact, toward the end of his epistle, James uses the term "Lord" in reference to the God of Israel (5:10-11) *directly following* his use of this term for Yeshua (5:7-8). Professor William R. Baker writes:

> The significance of James applying to Jesus the Septuagintal word for Yahweh who covenanted with Israel cannot be overstated. Yet, in doing this, James parallels what must have become common practice among early Christians, since the referencing Jesus as 'Lord' is commonplace in the NT. In shar-

2 Ibid., p. 52

> ing this title with God, James implies Jesus' share in the honor and respect which in Judaism was reserved for God alone.[3]

James also says there is only one "Judge" (4:11-12), clearly in reference to the one true God of the Scriptures, and yet applies this office to Yeshua several verses later (5:9), indicating that the one true Judge—the God of the Scriptures—is a plurality. Beyond James' epistle, the fact of God's plurality is even clearer. In the Tanakh, for instance, YHWH stated that He will share His glory with no other (Isaiah 42:8). Yet in the New Testament, the Son receives worship and glory along with the Father (Revelation 5:11-14). Either God changed His mind about not sharing His glory or the Son is one with the Father and equally God. Furthermore, John calls Yeshua "the true God" (1 John 5:20) and Paul prayed to the Father and the "Lord Yeshua" together (1 Thessalonians 3:11-13). If we want to get back to the faith of the original apostles, a big part of that means acknowledging the eternal divine nature of Messiah.

Sucking Up and Selling Out

Do you see all people the way God sees them—as precious children made in His image? Or do you view people only as a means to an end?

James wrote about how some people in the Messianic Community were sucking up to those who wore gold rings and fine clothing by giving them the best seats in the synagogue. Meanwhile, the poor people in the community were ignored, brushed aside, and told to sit on the floor. James rebukes these people for having "evil thoughts" (v.

---

3 William R. Baker, "Christology in the Epistle of James," *The Evangelical Quarterly 74.1* (Jan-Mar. 2002), pp. 47-57

4). They had a self-centered agenda to try to curry favor with the rich and socially important, which caused them to sell out their brothers and sisters in the Lord.

This partiality is anti-gospel. And yet, so-called believers engage in this type of behavior all the time. For instance, all too often believers will compromise their values in order to fit in with people of the world—the same people who mock and belittle their faith. James writes, "Are they not the ones who blaspheme the honorable name by which you were called?" (v. 7) Too often, because a Christian wants to be accepted by the cool and trendy secular crowd in their social scene, they'll hide their faith and sell out their integrity to get the praise and affirmation they crave from the very people who are against what they believe. It's a complete betrayal of Messiah.

For most of us, that's perhaps an extreme example of how we might violate this passage, but we show partiality in the church in other more subtle ways. For instance, some believers will discriminate against others on the basis of age. Younger people will sometimes treat older people as if they are out of touch and don't have anything useful to offer. After all, what can an older person teach you that you can't learn from a simple Google search? But the Torah says to honor the old man (Leviticus 19:32). Wisdom comes with age and experience, and young people do well to learn from their elders. On the other side of the coin, older people will sometimes treat younger people as if they are nothing but lazy and immature. But Paul tells Timothy, "Let no one despise you for your youth" (1 Timothy 4:12). Rather than honoring one another and treating each other with respect, we judge and create divisions within the body. We discriminate not only on the basis of age but also on the basis of gender, how we dress, religious traditions, etc. We're always finding reasons to avoid treating everyone with the love and respect that they deserve as people made in God's image.

We need to put our self-interest and prejudices aside and stop seeing people as just a means to an end. We need to stand firm in our faith and stop compromising for the sake of fitting in with the crowd. We need to stop creating man-made divisions among ourselves and get back to loving God and loving our neighbor.

Racism: A Demonic, Anti-Gospel Abomination

James warns us against "making distinctions" among ourselves and becoming "judges with evil thoughts" (v. 4). The most egregious violation of this biblical principle is racism. A racist is someone who discriminates against and hates certain people on the basis of the color of their skin. A racist also tends to think that their race is superior to that of others. Every person of every race is capable of being a racist, but a follower of Yeshua must not be one. If a racist claims to follow the Messiah, they are a liar. James says, "Show no partiality as you hold the faith in our Lord Jesus Christ, the Lord of glory" (v. 1). In other words, racism and faith in Yeshua are incompatible.

If that seems harsh, you'll need to take it up with the Scriptures. The Torah clearly states, "You shall not hate your brother in your heart" (Leviticus 19:17). Since racism is a form of hatred, it is a violation of the Torah, and thus sin. Moreover, according to 1 John 4:20, one who hates his brother *cannot* love God. The Messiah's Kingdom will be made up of people "from every nation, from all tribes and peoples and languages" (Revelation 7:9). Thus, the notion of one race being superior to another is contradicted by the Messianic Kingdom, in which all races of people exist as one people of God. Not only that, but our Messiah Himself commands us to pray for this Kingdom to come to earth (Matthew 6:10). Thus, the very prayer that Yeshua taught us to pray demands that we oppose racism.

Indeed, racists cannot be part of the Kingdom. They will go to hell unless they repent of their racism. As it says in John's first epistle, "Anyone who hates a brother or sister is a murderer, and you know that no murderer has eternal life residing in him" (1 John 3:15). As for followers of Yeshua, we are called to not only reject but also fiercely oppose racism.

CHAPTER 9

LOVE YOUR NEIGHBOR

If you really fulfill the royal law according to the Scripture, "You shall love your neighbor as yourself," you are doing well. But if you show partiality, you are committing sin and are convicted by the law as transgressors. For whoever keeps the whole law but fails in one point has become guilty of all of it. For he who said, "Do not commit adultery," also said, "Do not murder." If you do not commit adultery but do murder, you have become a transgressor of the law. So speak and so act as those who are to be judged under the law of liberty. For judgment is without mercy to one who has shown no mercy. Mercy triumphs over judgment.

James 2:8-13

In this passage, James continues to unpack the problem of partiality within the Messianic Community. He delves into how the royal law, "You shall love your neighbor as yourself," is the ultimate standard by which our actions are to be judged. That is to say, as long as the royal law serves as our foundation for everything we do, we "are doing well." James' point is that if you love your neighbor, you will not show partiality. You'll acknowledge that your poor brother is just as much your neighbor and therefore just as worthy of love and respect as your rich brother.

On the other hand, if you show partiality, you are sinning and have transgressed the Torah. James' argument in support of this position is quite simple: All of Torah is valid and authoritative. The God who said, "Do not commit adultery," is the same God who also said, "Do not murder." That is to say, if you've rejected the authority of one law, you've rejected it all. Even if you act religious in other ways, you must not think that you're then justified in showing partiality (or committing any other sin for that matter). From God's perspective, you are still a transgressor. Yeshua's rant against the Pharisees' religious hypocrisy comes to mind here:

> Woe to you, scribes and Pharisees, hypocrites! For you tithe mint and dill and cumin, and *have neglected the weightier matters of the law*: justice and mercy and faithfulness. These you ought to have done, *without neglecting the others*. (Matthew 23:23, emphasis added)

Like Yeshua, James is against the idea that we can just pick and choose which commandments are relevant to our lives. We have no authority to declare some commandments valid and others invalid. All of the Torah is important. Also like Yeshua, James teaches that love is the summation of the Torah. Proper Torah observance must flow from a heart of love for our neighbor. If we claim to be Torah observant but neglect matters of justice, mercy, and faithfulness, then we are not truly Torah observant. We are hypocrites. In fact, if love is not the guiding component of our Torah observance—if we are unmerciful towards those in need—we will be judged without mercy. Again, James' teaching here very clearly echoes the Sermon on the Mount. Yeshua said, "Blessed are the merciful, for they shall receive mercy" (Matthew 5:7). According to James, the mercy and kindness we extend toward others affects the mercy and kindness we receive. Followers of Yeshua ought to keep that in mind next time we are tempted to reject others or look down on them.

Every Iota and Dot of the Law

During His Sermon on the Mount, Yeshua made it clear that He didn't come to abolish the Torah and that every "iota" and "dot" still stands—even commandments regarding the Sabbath and dietary instructions. But why does God care about whether or not we rest on the seventh day or eat unclean animals? Is it that big of a deal? What do these things really have to do with being a Christian?

I'm blessed to have many intelligent and God-fearing Christian friends who often encourage and challenge me in my walk with the Messiah. As Christians, we share many beliefs in common, including the authority of Scripture. However, I have several disagreements with some of my friends on the interpretation and application of Scripture—namely, the relevance of certain parts of the Torah. In light of 1 John 2:6, which says we ought to walk as Yeshua walked, I believe our worship and obedience to our heavenly Father ought to reflect Yeshua's worship and obedience. So how did Yeshua walk? Professor of Biblical Literature, Dr. Brad Young, puts it this way:

> We too often view Jesus in a historical vacuum with the result that we transpose our twenty-first century Western values and concerns onto him. We tend to make him into a good Methodist, Catholic, Baptist, Anglican, Pentecostal, or whatever denominational orientation we may be. The historical Jesus remains a Jew. His faith and obedience to his Father in heaven had at its center the precious gift given at Mount Sinai: Torah.[1]

Since Yeshua lived a life of obedience to the Torah, we ought to revisit these things if we desire to "walk as He walked." Even though the Sabbath, festivals, and dietary instructions aren't really practiced by the majority of Christians today, these things were

---

1 Dr. Brad Young, *Meet the Rabbis: Rabbinic Thought and the Teachings of Jesus* (Grand Rapids, MI: Baker Academic, 2010), p. 46

important to Yeshua. Therefore, it should be important to us to learn how these commandments might apply to us today.

When I am challenged on my beliefs concerning the validity of some parts of the Torah, I'm usually confronted with arguments based on certain New Testament passages that are interpreted in such a way to dispute my beliefs. That's fine, and it's good to debate Scripture and to lovingly challenge each other on biblical grounds. However, after showing how the New Testament actually teaches us to keep the Sabbath, festivals, and dietary instructions, I sometimes find that the focus of the conversation drifts away from what the Bible says and moves toward *our* opinions with regard to the importance of such commandments.

One might ask, "What does eating pork or shrimp have to do with living a moral life for God? Aren't there more important things to worry about, like taking care of the poor?" It's true that some commandments are more important than others—the weightier matters of the Torah, as Yeshua puts it. We should do all we can to care for the poor. And indeed, acts of love and kindness toward our neighbor take precedence over other laws in the Torah. A good illustration to demonstrate this principle is Yeshua's parable of the good Samaritan (Luke 10:30-37). In the parable, the Priest and Levite determined that they could not help the wounded man on the side of the road. Why? Because in order to fulfill their responsibilities at the Temple, the Torah required them to be in a state of ritual purity, and helping the wounded man could have potentially made them ritually impure. But in not helping the man, they failed to love their neighbor and thus became transgressors of the Torah. The good Samaritan, on the other hand, showed love and mercy toward the man and thus fulfilled the Torah. We must not become so overly obsessed with the minute details of the Torah that we neglect the more important parts. However, we also must not say that the "less important" parts of the Torah aren't important at all. God forbid! While we certainly must emphasize the weightier matters of the Torah, at the same time we must not invalidate the lighter matters:

> Woe to you, scribes and Pharisees, hypocrites! For you tithe mint and dill and cumin, and have neglected the weightier matters of the law: justice and mercy and faithfulness. These you ought to have done, *without neglecting the others.* (Matthew 23:23, emphasis added)

> Therefore whoever relaxes *one of the least of these commandments* and teaches others to do the same will be called least in the kingdom of heaven, but *whoever does them and teaches them will be called great* in the kingdom of heaven. (Matthew 5:19, emphasis added)

When I first got married, I was surprised to discover all the "little things" that meant a great deal to my wife. To me, it wasn't that big of a deal to let the kitchen trash can overflow. "I'll take out the trash eventually," I would say to myself. In my days as a lazy bachelor, I could neglect to take out the trash for weeks and not even notice. My wife, on the other hand, did not appreciate having to stop in the middle of cooking dinner to remove a full trash bag just so she could make room! Therefore, out of love for my bride, I had to make a conscious effort to take out the trash. It's something that's important to her, and I want to honor her.

Now, is remembering to take out the trash as important as not committing adultery? Obviously not, but I've learned in my marriage that being faithful includes not only the big commitments but also the little ones. We should want to love and serve our spouse, and that means taking seriously the things that matter to them no matter how small. What if I continued not to care about the trash because I didn't think it was that big of a deal? Would I be showing my wife the love and respect due to her as my bride?

In the same way, several things are important to God. He had Moses write them down after He had delivered the Israelites from Egypt. And everyone who desired to follow God (including the strangers who sojourned with native Israel) had to agree to honor Him *in the way* He desires to be honored. God doesn't change. If obedience to God's commandments was important in the past, it is still important today. Moreover, it will be important in the future as well. For example, the feast of Sukkot is so important to God that He will mandate that all the nations celebrate it after Yeshua's Second Coming (Zechariah 14:16-19).

Aside from honoring God, keeping these often-neglected Torah commandments has a lot of practical benefits. For instance, God knows that we all need a day of rest. We weren't created to work constantly without a break. The Sabbath blesses us with physical rest. It takes us back to creation (Exodus 20:11) and reminds us of the hope we have in the Messianic Kingdom to come. It also reminds us of our deliverance from slavery in Egypt (Deuteronomy 5:15), which is a prophetic picture of our salvation in Yeshua who rescued us from the slavery of sin and death. Therefore, resting on the Sabbath is an opportunity to proclaim the Gospel by our simple obedience. Lastly, the Sabbath, along with all of God's festivals, emphasizes the value of community and identity as God's people (Exodus 31:13; Leviticus 23).

In regard to the dietary instructions, the practical benefits are obvious. It's simply not a good idea to eat a poisonous tree frog! Scientific studies have revealed potential health risks associated with eating pork and shellfish too. For instance, one study[2] found that the meat of unclean animals showed significantly higher levels of toxicity compared to the meat of clean animals. But God's dietary instructions have more to do with holiness than healthiness. In Leviticus 11:44—right in the middle of the dietary instructions—God says, "Be holy, for I am holy." This same standard of holiness is later reiterated to Christians by the apostle Peter (1 Peter 1:16). Following God's commandments, including His instructions on what not to eat, is an expression of loving Him with all our heart, mind, soul, and strength. This obedience is born out of a desire to be holy and set apart as His bride. And even if these commands have no practical benefit to them at all—if they're purely symbolic of living a life of holiness—so what? Christians believe in doing a lot of things for purely symbolic reasons. For instance, baptism has no practical benefit, but all Christians believe we should do it. Why? Because God said so.

At the end of the day, God expresses His will to us through His written word. Do we truly believe that? Because to say, "This commandment is irrelevant," is to say, "God's will for my life in this area isn't important to me." God is the one who makes the rules, not us. And if we desire to follow him, that includes following His rules. Christian theologian R.C. Sproul put it best: "When there's something in the Word of God that I don't like, the problem is not with the Word of God. It's with me."[3]

---

2 David I. Macht (1953), An Experimental Pharmacological Appreciation of Leviticus XI and Deuteronomy XIV. *Bulletin of the History of Medicine*, 27, John Hopkins University Press, pp. 444-450

3 Matt Smethurst, *The Gospel Coalition*. "40 Quotes from R. C. Sproul (1939-2017)." www.thegospelcoalition.com. Accessed 10/15/18

CHAPTER 10

PRACTICE LIVING FAITH

What good is it, my brothers, if someone says he has faith but does not have works? Can that faith save him? If a brother or sister is poorly clothed and lacking in daily food, and one of you says to them, "Go in peace, be warmed and filled," without giving them the things needed for the body, what good is that? So also faith by itself, if it does not have works, is dead. But someone will say, "You have faith and I have works." Show me your faith apart from your works, and I will show you my faith by my works. You believe that God is one; you do well. Even the demons believe—and shudder! Do you want to be shown, you foolish person, that faith apart from works is useless? Was not Abraham our father justified by works when he offered up his son Isaac on the altar? You see that faith was active along with his works, and faith was completed by his works; and the Scripture was fulfilled that says, "Abraham believed God, and it was counted to him as righteousness"—and he was called a friend of God. You see that a person is justified by works and not by faith alone. And in the same way was not also Rahab the prostitute justified by works when she received the messengers and sent them out by another way? For as the body apart from the spirit is dead, so also faith apart from works is dead.

James 2:14-26

At the beginning of the second chapter of his epistle, James defined faith in Yeshua the Messiah as something that is incompatible with partiality. According to James, followers of Yeshua who fulfill the royal law in the Torah—"You shall love your neighbor as yourself"—will not discriminate against the poor but instead will show mercy and kindness to everyone regardless of who they are. It's from that basis that James now extends his definition of faith in Yeshua to include works: "Faith by itself, if it does not have works, is dead" (v. 17). That is to say, faith is not merely affirming the truth of biblical doctrines, such as equality and fairness, but actively living out those beliefs. If we claim to have faith in Yeshua but don't do the works that ought to flow from faith, then our faith is illegitimate—a counterfeit. James gives a specific example of this counterfeit faith: neglecting to help someone in their time of need. This is a direct violation of the Torah, which instructs us to open our hand to the needy:

> If among you, one of your brothers should become poor, in any of your towns within your land that the Lord your God is giving you, you shall not harden your heart or shut your hand against your poor brother, but you shall open your hand to him and lend him sufficient for his need, whatever it may be. (Deuteronomy 15:7-8).

Instead of actively caring for the brother or sister in need, the religious hypocrite in James' example says, "Go in peace, be warmed and filled," without doing anything to meet their real needs. "What good is that?" asks James. He is bewildered by the neglect for the poor within the Messianic community. How is it *even possible* to call yourself a follower of Yeshua and neglect to help someone in need? The apostle John shares this sentiment:

> But if anyone has the world's goods and sees his brother in need, yet closes his heart against him, *how does God's love abide in him*? Little children, let us not love in word or talk but in deed and in truth. (1 John 3:17-18, emphasis added)

James uses the word *nekros*, "dead," to describe this type of counterfeit faith. It is like a lifeless body (v. 26). He also describes it as being powerless to save (v. 14) and "useless" (v. 20). To James, it is incomprehensible that someone can claim to have faith in Yeshua and not follow through with what such a faith requires. After all, if mere mental assent to certain biblical truths was sufficient, even the demons would be justified. The demons mentioned in Mark's gospel, for example, clearly affirmed that Yeshua was "the Holy One of God" (Mark 1:24), but their belief in that truth alone was not true saving faith. Indeed, affirming that "God is one," as it says in the *shema* (Deuteronomy 6:4)—a foundational confession recited daily in Judaism—necessarily involves a commitment to keep God's commandments (Deuteronomy 6:5-9). A saving faith is a belief that leads to good works. If someone claims to have faith but that faith is not evidenced by works, then, as this passage from James strongly implies, they don't actually have saving faith. This teaching again echoes Yeshua's Sermon on the Mount:

> "Not everyone who says to me, 'Lord, Lord' will enter the kingdom of heaven, but the one who does the will of my Father who is in heaven." (Matthew 7:21)

To clarify, this is not to say that humans can earn their salvation by doing good deeds or keeping certain commandments. Scripture is abundantly clear in other places that salvation is a free gift of God received through faith, not the result of human effort (e.g. Ephesians 2:8-9). James is simply emphasizing that doing good works is the necessary outgrowth of saving faith. The bottom line is that true faith *will* produce good works. An authentic follower of the Messiah *will* reflect the love of Yeshua in their character and deeds. This word from James is designed to cause us to look at ourselves and make sure we are actually living in accordance to what we believe—and if we aren't, we need to wake up and get our act together.

James expounds on this point by citing the biblical examples of Abraham and Rahab. In regard to Abraham, his faith initially consisted of simply believing God: "And he believed the Lord, and he counted it to him as righteousness" (Genesis 15:6). As Abraham followed God, his faith was evidenced by his obedience to God, eventually culminating to his offering up Isaac on the altar. Abraham's faith was "completed"—that is, brought to its intended goal—by his works. That's why, when God later confirms the Abrahamic promise to Isaac, it is "because Abraham obeyed my voice and kept my charge, my commandments, my statutes, and my laws" (Genesis 26:5). James' second biblical example is Rahab. She demonstrated her faith by showing hospitality to the Israelite spies in the city of Jericho and even saving their lives. She had come to believe in the God of Israel by hearing the stories about how God had delivered them from Egypt, split the Red Sea, and defeated the two Amorite kings (Joshua 2:8-13). This belief compelled her to *do* something. Thus, her faith was shown by her works to be a true saving faith.

James has pointed out repeatedly that true faith in Yeshua is much more than merely believing in God. It's much more than simply affirming the truth of certain biblical doctrines. After all, "even the demons believe—and shudder!" (v. 19) The bottom line is this: If we want to have an authentic, living faith, something more than mere intellectual belief is required. We must follow through with what our faith in Yeshua requires and be doers of the word.

James vs. Paul?

When reading through James' and Paul's writings in the New Testament, Bible readers are inevitably confronted with a big problem: James and Paul appear to contradict each other concerning a significant doctrine. That is, are we justified—"saved"—by faith alone or by faith in addition to works? James and Paul give seemingly conflicting answers. For instance, James says, "You see that a person is justified by works and not by faith alone" (v. 24). But Paul says, "For by grace you have been saved through faith. And this is not your own doing; it is the gift of God, not a result of works, so that no one may boast" (Ephesians 2:8-9).

Do James and Paul present opposing views on justification? Not if we believe the Scriptures to be God-breathed (2 Timothy 3:16). If the Bible is the written word of God, then every word of it is true. Therefore, it does not contradict itself. That isn't to say that we won't encounter difficulties in the text or that we'll always be able to resolve every issue. But that's not the fault of God's word; it's the fault of our limitations as humans. While the Bible is God's special revelation, that revelation is expressed through human language, which is limited. Human language can be ambiguous and therefore subject to misinterpretation. John Piper puts this point well:

> The inspiration of the Word of God is like the incarnation of the Son of God. When the Son of God became a human being he became vulnerable to abuse and death. When the Word of God became human language, it became vulnerable to ambiguity and misunderstanding.[1]

With that said, our duty as believers is to wrestle with the text and do our best to resolve any difficulties we encounter so that we can have a clear understanding of the consistent message of the Scriptures. As the apostle Paul has instructed us, "Do your best to present yourself

---

1 John Piper, *desiringGod*. "Does James Contradict Paul?" www.desiringgod.org. Accessed 10/25/18

to God as one approved, a worker who has no need to be ashamed, rightly handling the word of truth" (2 Timothy 2:15). So how might we reconcile this apparent contradiction between James and Paul?

The first thing to note is that James is not denying the fact that we're justified by faith. He doesn't teach that faith can't save; he teaches that *counterfeit faith* can't save. What is this counterfeit faith? It's the kind of "faith" that might intellectually affirm certain biblical truths but doesn't lead to good works. True saving faith is fully surrendering to Yeshua. It's committing your whole life to Him, not only in word but also in deed. It's a commitment to follow Yeshua daily: "If anyone would come after me, let him deny himself and take up his cross daily and follow me" (Luke 9:23). So James agrees with Paul that we are saved by faith, but faith needs to be defined correctly. James simply emphasizes that doing good works is the necessary outgrowth of saving faith. "Faith" that doesn't produce good works is a counterfeit.

The second thing to note is that Paul taught the same thing as James—that is, true saving faith is evidenced by works. That's the type of faith that justifies us. Ephesians 2:8-9 was quoted earlier, saying, "By grace you have been saved through faith [...] not a result of works." But when we look at the very next verse, we see that Paul clearly affirms that this saving faith will result in good works: "For we are his workmanship, created in Christ Jesus *for good works*, which God prepared beforehand, *that we should walk in them*" (Ephesians 2:10, emphasis added). Indeed, we see this expressed throughout Paul's letters: Yeshua redeemed us so that we would be "zealous for good works" (Titus 2:14); believers are to "be careful to devote themselves to good works" (Titus 3:8); Christian women should adorn themselves "with good works" (1 Timothy 2:10); wealthy believers are to seek to "be rich in good works" (1 Timothy 6:18). These are just a few of many examples.

In summary, James and Paul agree that we're saved by God's grace through faith, not by our own effort. Nothing we do can earn us God's favor. James says "we all stumble in many ways" (James 3:2), clearly affirming that all of us are guilty of sin and have fallen short of God's glory. We need a Savior. Yeshua the Messiah was sent to pay the price for our redemption so that we can be forgiven and justified. And when we receive Yeshua as our Savior through faith, that is the basis of our salvation. But as John Calvin once said, "It is therefore faith alone which justifies, and yet the faith which justifies is not alone."[2] Good works are the outgrowth of true saving faith, as both James and Paul affirm.

Would James Consider You A Christian?

According to a 2017 Gallup poll,[3] about three-quarters of Americans say they identify with a Christian faith. Forty-eight percent of those who identify as Christian are classified as part of a "Protestant/Other Christian" group. (Catholics and Mormons make up the other part of the overall "Christian" percentage.) However, among Americans affiliated with the Protestant/Other Christian groups, only fifty percent are classified as "highly religious" according to the poll. Thirty-four percent are classified as "moderately religious," and sixteen percent are "not religious." The religiosity results are based on self-reports of those interviewed when they were asked about church attendance and the importance of religion in their lives.

What might we infer from these poll results? Well, as harsh as it sounds, many Americans who see themselves as Christians perhaps

---

2 John Calvin, *Acts of the Council of Trent with the Antidote* (Lance George Marshall, 2011)

3 Frank Newport, *Gallup*. "2017 Update on Americans and Religion." news.gallup.com. Accessed 10/30/18

aren't really Christians at all—at least not in any meaningful way. While three-quarters of Americans identify as part of the Christian faith, apparently a high percentage of them don't consider their faith to be that important. They believe God exists, but their life doesn't reflect that belief. The problem is that you can't be a "moderately religious" Christian according to the Bible. Such a thing doesn't exist. Apathy is not a fruit of the Spirit.

The word *Christian* has an actual meaning. It literally means "follower of Christ." What does it mean to follow Christ? Well, it's much more than simply having pleasant feelings toward Christ and sharing inspirational Bible quotes on Facebook from time to time. Yeshua said, "If anyone would come after me, let him deny himself and take up his cross daily and follow me" (Luke 9:23). Thus, following Christ entails denying yourself. It requires you to surrender—daily—to God's will and plan. It requires sacrifice, courage, holiness, and being willing to face persecution for doing what's right. It requires you to love God with your entire being and love your neighbor as yourself.

Many people think they're Christians since they once recited a prayer to ask Jesus into their hearts. Since they said a magic prayer, they're safe from damnation and can therefore ignore God and live their lives as they please. Maybe they'll think about God every once in a while, attend Church occasionally, listen to Christian music, and pray before meals (when they remember). But most of the time, to them, God is some distant cosmic Santa Claus they profess to believe in just in case hell is actually real. Obviously this type of "faith" expressed by many who claim to be Christians is not true faith.

Imagine a husband treating his wife the way many Christians in America treat God. He says he loves her but ignores her for most of their marriage. He isn't devoted to her and doesn't actively pursue her daily—is that really love? Can you really call such a relationship a "marriage"? Technically, yes, but not in any meaningful way. It would be a marriage in name only. The same is true of Christians whose lives are not devoted to their Messiah. Their claim to be a Christian is baseless. It's a meaningless label. As James has asked, "What good is it, my brothers, if someone says he has faith but does not have works? Can that faith save him?" (v. 14) The answer is no.

CHAPTER 11

SPEAK LIFE

Not many of you should become teachers, my brothers, for you know that we who teach will be judged with greater strictness. For we all stumble in many ways. And if anyone does not stumble in what he says, he is a perfect man, able also to bridle his whole body. If we put bits into the mouths of horses so that they obey us, we guide their whole bodies as well. Look at the ships also: though they are so large and are driven by strong winds, they are guided by a very small rudder wherever the will of the pilot directs. So also the tongue is a small member, yet it boasts of great things. How great a forest is set ablaze by such a small fire! And the tongue is a fire, a world of unrighteousness. The tongue is set among our members, staining the whole body, setting on fire the entire course of life, and set on fire by hell. For every kind of beast and bird, of reptile and sea creature, can be tamed and has been tamed by mankind, but no human being can tame the tongue. It is a restless evil, full of deadly poison. With it we bless our Lord and Father, and with it we curse people who are made in the likeness of God. From the same mouth come blessing and cursing. My brothers, these things ought not to be so. Does a spring pour forth from the same opening both fresh and salt water? Can a fig tree, my brothers, bear olives, or a grapevine produce figs? Neither can a salt pond yield fresh water.

James 3:1-12

What does being a follower of Yeshua really mean? So far James has explained that true believers are steadfast in the midst of trials. They are not controlled by their anger. They are "doers of the word," and their Torah observance flows from a heart of love for their neighbor. They do not show partiality, but they recognize that everyone is made in the image of God and therefore worthy of honor and respect. And finally, their faith works. That is to say, their lives are fully devoted to the Messiah and they actively pursue righteousness. Now James reveals another aspect of what it means to be a follower of Yeshua. He says, "If anyone does not stumble in what he says, he is a perfect man, able also to bridle his whole body" (v. 2). This idea of being "perfect" goes back to the concept introduced in James 1:4—"And let steadfastness have its full effect, that you may be perfect and complete, lacking in nothing." Being perfect refers to being spiritually mature. Thus, growing in spiritual maturity as a follower of Yeshua the Messiah entails learning how to control your speech.

James begins this chapter with a warning: "Not many of you should become teachers, my brothers, for you know that we who teach will be judged with greater strictness" (v. 1). Is James discouraging believers from becoming teachers within the community? Essentially yes. Teachers have an enormous impact on a community, and that influence can potentially lead to massive spiritual destruction if that influence is abused. Scot McKnight explains it this way:

> It is the status of a teacher that leads James to turn toward them. He prohibits the rise in numbers of teachers because of the abuse of the teaching position with irresponsible speech [...] The fundamental problem is that these teachers, who explained God's Word and God's ways for the messianic community and who brought "a new insight into an old word from God" could also abuse that vulnerable charismatic authority by saying the wrong thing at the wrong time to the wrong persons or about another person and so lead to the destruction of the delicate relationships that characterize the Christian community.[1]

---

1 Scot McKnight, *The New International Commentary of the New Testament: The Letter of James* (Grand Rapids, MI: Wm. B. Eerdmans Publishing Co., 2011), p. 271

In other words, real lives are at stake. Ultimately James is trying to emphasize the weightiness of being in a position of authority and encourage those who desire to become teachers, as well as those who currently hold that position, to take it seriously. As he says, teachers will be "judged with greater strictness." Why? Because "to whom much was given, of him much will be required" (Luke 12:48). Teachers have been given a gift of knowledge and influence beyond other members in the community, and therefore they have a responsibility to use their gift to help others grow in their knowledge and relationship with the Lord.

James' warning is important because there is often a temptation to abuse power and authority for selfish gain. Yeshua called out the Pharisees for this very thing. The Pharisees loved the place of honor at feasts and the best seats in the synagogue. They loved being called "rabbi" by others (Matthew 23:6-11). And their position of influence unfortunately presented many opportunities to cause chaos in their communities through their hypocrisy and false teaching. They didn't truly care for the people; they cared only about being seen as superior to others. This problem isn't exclusive to teachers and leaders. Indeed, "we all stumble in many ways" (v. 2). But when teachers stumble, they can potentially cause an entire community to be torn apart. If you do not take seriously the impact your words and actions have on others, you should not be a teacher.

While James specifically addresses teachers in this passage, that certainly doesn't excuse the rest of us from the responsibility of controlling our speech. As J.K. McKee points out,[2] James previously gave a general admonition to everyone regarding this same issue: "Let

---

2 J.K. McKee, *James for the Practical Messianic* (Richardson, TX: Messianic Apologetics, 2013), p. 86

every person be quick to hear, slow to speak, slow to anger" (James 1:19, emphasis added). So we can all be challenged and learn from what James has to say here. The tongue is a powerful tool that can be used to bring either glory to God or chaos and destruction. As it says in Proverbs, "Death and life are in the power of the tongue, and those who love it will eat its fruits" (Proverbs 18:21).

James' first two analogies—bits in the mouths of horses and rudders on ships—demonstrate the massive effect that our words can have on others. Just like a small bit can guide a large horse and a small rudder can guide the whole ship, the tongue is a "small member" that has the potential to influence an entire community toward destruction. It "boasts of great things" (v. 5). McKnight suggests that this boasting is "most likely the arrogant and divisive warmongering on the part of some of the teachers and leaders in the messianic community."[3] According to Craig Keener, "Many popular teachers urged that revolt was the only solution to current problems."[4] James seemed to be concerned that irresponsible leaders could misuse their influence to incite the entire community to take violent action against their oppressors, which would be directly contrary to Yeshua's message that we ought to be peacemakers (Matthew 5:9; James 3:18).

This leads to James' third analogy: "How great a forest is set ablaze by such a small fire!" (v. 5) James wants his readers, especially the teachers and leaders, to understand that their words have the potential to destroy them and the entire community. Just as a fire can cause great destruction to a forest, careless words and false teachings

---

3 Scot McKnight, *The New International Commentary of the New Testament: The Letter of James* (Grand Rapids, MI: Wm. B. Eerdmans Publishing Co., 2011), pp. 279-280

4 Craig Keener, *NIV Cultural Backgrounds Study Bible: Bringing to Life the Ancient World of Scripture*, James 3:13-18 (Grand Rapids, MI: Zondervan, 2016)

can hurt many people. James says the tongue is "set on fire by hell" (v. 6). That is to say, the source of evil speech comes right out of hell—and that's exactly where it leads as well! The Greek word for "hell" is *Gehenna*, which refers to the Hinnom Valley southwest of Jerusalem. This valley was a place where apostate Israelites burned their children as human sacrifices to Molech (2 Kings 23:10; 2 Chronicles 28:3; Jeremiah 7:31). In the New Testament, this word is used as a metaphor for the place of everlasting punishment reserved for sinners (e.g. Mark 9:43). James' point is that uncontrolled speech brings about chaos, destruction, and death. That's all it can do, because the tongue is set on fire by hell itself.

James goes on to say that humans made in God's image are able to tame, and have tamed, every kind of animal (Genesis 1:26). And yet, shockingly, nobody can tame the wild animal of the tongue. James calls the tongue a "restless evil, full of deadly poison" (v. 8), capturing the same imagery in the psalms: "They make their tongue sharp as a serpent's, and under their lips is the venom of asps" (Psalm 140:3). It should be noted what James doesn't say. He doesn't say that the tongue cannot be tamed; he says "no human being" can tame it. At least not by our own strength. It is only possible when we "receive with meekness the implanted word" (James 1:21) through the work of the Holy Spirit, which will empower us to have self-control. In other words, only God can tame the human tongue.

James shines a light on the hypocrisy of believers in regard to their speech: With their tongue they both bless the Lord and curse people made in the image of God. "These things ought not to be so," says James (v. 10). Blessing God while cursing your neighbor is a contradiction, like a spring pouring forth both fresh and salt water or a fig tree bearing olives or a grapevine producing figs. The point that James is making here is the same point Yeshua made during His

Sermon on the Mount: "A healthy tree cannot bear bad fruit, nor can a diseased tree bear good fruit" (Matthew 7:18). Ultimately our words reveal who we really are: "What comes out of the mouth proceeds from the heart" (Matthew 15:18). Evil speech is incompatible with faith in Yeshua the Messiah. If someone consistently curses their neighbor and exercises zero control over their words, then perhaps they don't truly have faith in Yeshua. Indeed, if we cannot bridle our tongue, our religion is worthless (James 1:26).

So much of the pain and chaos we experience in life is the result of our lack of self-control over our speech. Our prayer ought to be, "Set a guard, O Lord, over my mouth; keep watch over the door of my lips!" (Psalm 141:3) We cannot take this lightly.

Five Characteristics of a False Teacher

James admonishes teachers to control their speech and to be thoughtful in what they say. Because of the influence they have on others, they will be "judged with greater strictness" (v. 1). But the people also have a duty to be discerning so that they are not led astray by false teaching. We are told in 1 John to "test" the message of a teacher or prophet to see if what they say is truly from God. The reason is that "many false prophets have gone out into the world (1 John 4:1)." Yeshua said that we will recognize false prophets by their fruits (Matthew 7:15-20). What are some of the identifying marks of a false prophet or teacher?

The best way to recognize a counterfeit is to be familiar with the real thing. A Federal agent doesn't become an expert in identifying counterfeit money by studying counterfeit bills. He first studies genuine money until he becomes so familiar with the real thing that he can easily tell the difference between genuine and counterfeit bills. In the same way, the best way to avoid being deceived by a false message is to study and know the true message as taught in the Scriptures. The Bible itself stands as the final authority against which everything else is to be measured. As Messianic theologian Tim Hegg says, "A person determines if a stick is crooked by putting it next to a straight stick. Let the Bible be your straight stick."[5]

As we meditate on God's word day and night, we become like a tree planted by streams of water—firmly established in the truth (Psalm 1). We as followers of Yeshua ought to know the Scriptures so well that when a teacher or prophet gives a false message, we will be able to clearly recognize it as such. Having said that, the Scriptures plainly outline the characteristics of false prophets and teachers that we ought to look out for. This section will examine five of those characteristics.

The first and most obvious way to tell if someone if a false prophet is if they prophesy falsely. The Torah says that we are not to revere the one who speaks in the name of the Lord presumptuously (Deuteronomy 18:22). That is to say, if someone claims to speak in the name of the Lord and they declare that something will occur in the future but it doesn't come to pass, then we are to disregard their teachings.

Sadly, a great number of false prophets are leading many astray in our days. You'll often find them on the Internet claiming to have discovered some secret knowledge embedded in the Scriptures and making sensational predictions, setting specific dates for the Second Coming of Messiah and other end times events. These types of "prophetic" predictions have a zero percent success rate and serve only to profane the name of God and make believers look foolish. Speculating about end times events in the Bible is not necessarily wrong, but we need to be on guard the moment someone starts claim-

---

5 Tim Hegg, *TorahResource*. "The Battle for the Bible: Are the Inspired Scriptures Enough?" www.torahresource.com. Accessed 11/7/18

ing to be some kind of authority and making bold future predictions about specific dates and times. According to the Bible, prophecy is not something to be taken lightly.

A second characteristic of a false teacher is that they encourage believers to abandon God's ways. Even if someone gives a prophecy and it comes to pass, they still might be a false prophet. According to Deuteronomy 13:1-5, if a prophet tries to convince you to "leave the way in which the Lord your God commanded you to walk," you are not to listen to their words. Indeed, the main sign of a prophet of God is not whether they make accurate predictions or perform signs and wonders, but that their message conforms to the word of God. False teachers who speak against clear commandments of God abound in our day and age. Heretical teachers have written best-selling books and have given lectures to thousands of people in which they affirm same-sex "marriage" and encourage believers to abandon clear biblical boundaries regarding sexual morality. Sadly, these teachers are the ones being featured on popular talk shows as they misrepresent biblical Christianity and lead many people astray. We need to beware of these false teachers and not be afraid to call them out as the wolves they are.

A third characteristic of a false teacher is that they distort or minimize the Gospel message. An entire book of the Bible—the book of Galatians—is dedicated to defending the Gospel against false teachers who were attempting to pervert the true message (Galatians 1:7). The apostle Paul spends considerable time exposing the false doctrine that salvation by grace through faith in Yeshua wasn't enough. Paul's harsh judgment against those who taught that something more was needed of the Gentiles before they could be included in the community of God's people—namely that they first needed to get circumcised (Acts 15:1)—demonstrates the utmost importance of upholding the purity of the Gospel.

This false doctrine that Paul addresses in Galatians was destructive in two ways. It distorted not only the message of the Gospel but also the true purpose of the Torah. By teaching a gospel of works, the false teachers addressed in Galatians were misusing the Torah and forcing it to be something that God never intended it to be. The Torah was never designed to save anyone. Dr. Daniel Block explains:

> Paul seems to have functioned as a second Moses, not only in providing a profoundly theological interpretation of God's saving actions in Christ, but also in reminding his readers that salvation comes by grace alone. In Romans and Galatians his argumentation addresses those who would pervert the "law" (a narrow legalistic interpretation of Hebrew *Torah*) into a means of salvation, rather than treating it as a response to salvation as Moses perceived it. While on the surface Paul's responses to this heresy often appear to contradict Moses, these statements should be interpreted in context and as rhetorical responses to his opponents. In his own disposition toward the "law" he was in perfect step with Moses: obedience to the law was not a means for gaining salvation but a willing and grateful response to salvation already received.[6]

Having made that point, we could perhaps say that one of the identifying marks of a false teacher is that they consistently stress other biblical doctrines, whatever they may be, at the expense of the Gospel.

---

6 Daniel I. Block, *The Gospel According to Moses: Theological and Ethical Reflections on the Book of Deuteronomy* (Eugene, OR: Cascade Books, 2012), p. 3

For instance, as beautiful as the Torah is, and as much as the Scriptures support its ongoing authority in the lives of believers, it doesn't save you or make you righteous. This is not to diminish the value of the Torah but to elevate the Gospel to its rightful place. The Gospel is central to our faith as Christians and Messianics, and we must beware of anyone who leaves it behind.

A fourth characteristic of a false teacher is an obsession over foolish controversies. According to Paul in 1 Timothy 1:3-7, false teachers lack understanding of the Scriptures and sound theology. Therefore, they "devote themselves to myths" and drag people into "vain discussion." In a number of places in the New Testament, such as 2 Timothy 2:16, we are told to stay away from "pointless discussions." Why? "For people will become more and more ungodly." Thus, a false teacher who constantly promotes foolish controversies leads people into ungodly behavior.

Foolish controversies do "no good" and they "ruin those who listen" (2 Timothy 2:14). They are "unprofitable and worthless" (Titus 3:9). Instead of focusing on foolish controversies that have no value, Paul encourages us to "pursue righteousness, faith, love, and peace" (2 Timothy 2:22). James warns us about the damage that careless speech can cause in the believing community (vv. 1-12). Today, a lot of damage is caused by the careless speech of false teachers who obsessively promote conspiracy theories and "secret knowledge," leading to strife and division within the body (2 Timothy 2:23). We're warned to stay away from people who cause division because they "do not serve our Lord Christ, but their own appetites, and by smooth talk and flattery they deceive the hearts of the naïve" (Romans 16:17). Conspiracy theories such as Flat Earthism, secret codes embedded in Hebrew "word pictures," reptilian shapeshifter stories, UFOs, KJV-Onlyism, etc., offer no value to the lives of believers and are mere distractions from what we should be focused on. Teachers attempting to shove this theological junk food down the throats of the masses ought to be avoided.

A fifth characteristic of a false teacher is that they are selfish and opportunistic. James warns against "selfish ambition" among teachers (3:14-16). Sadly, many today hold the office of "teacher" not out of love and care for the people of God but for self-serving reasons. The prophet Micah describes false priests and prophets as those who "teach for a price" and "practice divination for money" (Micah 3:11). False teachers appear to be concerned only with entertaining the flock in order to achieve their own selfish gain, whether that be money, fame, power, or whatever. False teachers don't truly care about instructing believers in the ways of God. They see ministry simply as an opportunity to make a buck. If you notice a teacher consistently promoting themselves and serving himself rather than promoting Messiah and ministering to the needs of the people, flee from them.

May we discipline ourselves in the study of the Scriptures so that we can easily recognize the counterfeits when we see them. Yeshua said, "You will recognize them by their fruits" (Matthew 7:16). We must be on guard against false teachers and prophets so that we are not led astray and so we can warn others.

Lashon Hara: The Dangers of Evil Speech

Many are familiar with the children's rhyme, "Sticks and stones may break my bones, but words can never hurt me." While it's a catchy saying, the truth is that most of us would probably rather be assaulted with actual sticks and stones than be the victims of gossip and slander. Indeed, bruises inflicted on the body seem to heal much quicker than bruises inflicted on the soul. Few things are more painful than having your reputation destroyed due to *lashon hara*.

Lashon hara—that is, "evil speech"—can be understood simply as talking in such a way that disparages people in the eyes of others. In other words, the effect of lashon hara is humiliation. Most people who commit lashon hara likely don't realize just how much pain they cause their victims—for instance, most of the time we don't have malicious intentions when we gossip about others; we're just speaking carelessly—but studies[7] have shown that humiliation causes immense psychological damage. Humiliation is felt more intensely than even anger and happiness. The intense agony from humiliation has driven countless people to hurt themselves and others. This is not something to take lightly. Our words have the power to bring forth life or death (Proverbs 18:21).

As followers of Yeshua, we have a responsibility to control our speech. The Torah says, "You shall not go around as a slanderer among your people" (Leviticus 19:16). The principle of this commandment is reflected also in the New Testament: "Let no corrupting talk come out of your mouths, but only such as is good for building up" (Ephesians 4:29). James goes so far as to say that our religion is worthless if we do not bridle our tongue (1:26). Nevertheless, lashon hara seems to be an epidemic, even within the Church. And with the rise of social media making it possible for hurtful rumors to go "viral," it's all the more imperative that believers be on guard.

So how do we fight against this sin? First, we must acknowledge that lashon hara is indeed a sin. We need to stop attempting to justify ourselves in our minds when we engage in it. We might be tempted to mitigate our guilt when we speak evil against others, deluding ourselves into thinking it's not that big of a deal. But Yeshua and the apostles

---

7 Marte Otten & Kai J. Jonas (2013). *Humiliation as an Intense Emotional Experience: Evidence from the Elctro-Encephalogram*, Social neuroscience.

didn't share that perspective. To them, this was far from a light matter. Yeshua said we will one day give an account for every careless word we've spoken (Matthew 12:36). Therefore, we must see this sin for what it is—a deadly and contagious virus with the potential to destroy an entire community. We must resist the urge not only to engage in gossip and slander but also to listen to it. This might require that we, for example, boldly speak up when someone is gossiping and inform them that we cannot participate in such talk. Or it might require that we disconnect with certain people on social media. We ought to do whatever we need to in order to avoid participating in this sin.

Next, we must make a conscious effort to speak life about others. "Therefore encourage one another and build one another up" (1 Thessalonians 5:11). When we're tempted to speak evil against someone in front of others or online, we ought to instead use our words to praise and honor them. Training ourselves to speak life when we are tempted to speak death not only blocks evil speech but also actively fights against it. A community that is dedicated to building each other up with their words will be healthy, strong, and therefore a mighty force for Messiah's Kingdom in the world.

Ultimately, lashon hara is not a tongue problem but a heart problem. Yeshua said, "What comes out of the mouth proceeds from the heart" (Matthew 15:18). May the Father write His Torah on our hearts, empowering us to bridle our tongue. May we be moved to love and show mercy toward our neighbor, always seeking to build them up rather than tear them down. And may the Messiah truly be glorified in everything that we do and say.

CHAPTER 12

WALK IN WISDOM

Who is wise and understanding among you? By his good conduct let him show his works in the meekness of wisdom. But if you have bitter jealousy and selfish ambition in your hearts, do not boast and be false to the truth. This is not the wisdom that comes down from above, but is earthly, unspiritual, demonic. For where jealousy and selfish ambition exist, there will be disorder and every vile practice. But the wisdom from above is first pure, then peaceable, gentle, open to reason, full of mercy and good fruits, impartial and sincere. And a harvest of righteousness is sown in peace by those who make peace.

James 3:13-18

In this passage, James is still specifically addressing teachers and leaders within the community, but his teaching here really applies to all believers. Throughout his epistle, James has been describing what a true follower of Messiah looks like by contrasting authentic faith with religious hypocrisy. A true follower of Messiah practices religion that is pure and undefiled; a religious hypocrite's religion is worthless. A true follower of Messiah possesses a living faith; a religious hypocrite's faith is dead. Now James moves on to another aspect of what it means to be a genuine follower of Messiah: having wisdom from above.

The qualities of authentic faith in Messiah are made manifest in how we live. Pure and undefiled religion consists of bridling our tongue and caring for the widows and orphans. Living faith produces good works and obedience to God. Likewise, wisdom from above is expressed in meekness and good conduct. When James asked who was "wise and understanding" (v. 13), his readers would have immediately connected that back to the Torah:

> See, I have taught you statutes and rules, as the Lord my God commanded me, that you should do them in the land that you are entering to take possession of it. Keep them and do them, for that will be your *wisdom and your understanding* in the sight of the peoples, who, when they hear all these statutes, will say, "Surely this great nation is a *wise and understanding* people." (Deuteronomy 4:5-6, emphasis added)

How we live according to God's commandments will demonstrate whether or not we are wise and understanding. Thus, true wisdom is not merely theoretical but behavioral. However, doing good works is not all that is required—good works must be done in meekness or humility. This is in contrast to an "earthly, unspiritual, demonic" kind of wisdom (v. 15). This counterfeit wisdom does not flow from meekness but rather "bitter jealousy and selfish ambition" in the heart (v. 14). "Jealousy" in this passage is translated from the Greek *zelon*, which is derived from *zelos*. *Zelos* is often translated into English as "zeal." According to scholar David Nystrom, this word "can bear a negative nuance, often depicting some overblown and therefore inappropriate sense of devotion to God."[1] In James' day, many wanted to resort to violence in order to try to overthrow Roman rule, and they thought that such violence was perhaps religiously justified. This bitter jealousy coupled with a self-serving agenda results in "disorder and every vile practice" (v. 16). It does nothing to edify

1 David Nystrom, *The NIV Application Commentary: James* (Grand Rapids, MI: Zondervan, 1997). EPUB: James 3:13-18, para. 13

the community; it brings only confusion, strife, and division. Believers, especially teachers, need to examine our hearts to make sure we are not motivated by bitter jealousy and selfish ambition. James says, "Do not boast and be false to the truth" (v. 14). That is to say, stop pretending to be wise and understanding when you are fueled by such evil and demonic impulses. If we discover that we indeed have impure motives, we need to be honest with ourselves, repent, and ask God for true wisdom.

After warning us about counterfeit wisdom, James moves on to describe what wisdom from above looks like. As mentioned earlier, this true wisdom is expressed in good works flowing from meekness. James now outlines several attributes of true wisdom. First, wisdom from above is "pure." This is translated from the Greek *hagne*, which, according to MacArthur, "implies sincere, moral, spiritual character [...] it has more to do with a spiritual integrity, a moral sincerity, free from bitter jealousy, free from selfish ambition, free from arrogant self-promotion."[2] In other words, wisdom from above is first marked by a pure and sincere motive to honor God. It is not double-minded or selfish.

Second, wisdom from above is "peaceable," meaning peace-loving, free from strife and disorder. Yeshua said, "Blessed are the peacemakers, for they shall be called sons of God" (Matthew 5:9). Indeed, followers of Yeshua are characterized by a love for peace, not chaos and confusion.

Third, wisdom from above is "gentle." Paul uses this word in his list of qualifications for leaders within the congregation: "Therefore an overseer must be above reproach, the husband of one wife, sober-mind-

---

2 John MacArthur, *Grace to You*. "Earthly and Heavenly Wisdom, Part 3." www.gty.org. Accessed 11/15/18

ed, self-controlled, respectable, hospitable, able to teach, not a drunkard, not violent but *gentle*, not quarrelsome, not a lover of money" (1 Timothy 3:2-3, emphasis added). According to Nystrom, this word is "usually associated with justice, especially with the administration of justice, and suggests someone who does not abuse a position of power, but remains calm and sober and true to the highest ideals of such a position."[3] This attribute of wisdom entails humility, kindness, and judging righteously.

Fourth, wisdom from above is "open to reason." Wise believers must be teachable, clear thinking, and willing to listen and adjust their views when necessary. They assess the evidence as objectively as possible and humbly submit to the truth when it is made evident.

Fifth, wisdom from above is "full of mercy and good fruits." This is a deep love and concern for your neighbor expressed through good works. Yeshua said, "Blessed are the merciful, for they shall receive mercy" (Matthew 5:7).

Sixth, wisdom from above is "impartial and sincere." Wise believers do not show partiality (James 2:1-7)—that is, they judge fairly and truthfully. They are genuine, not hypocritical.

Exercising wisdom from above results in righteousness and peace. In other words, those who are committed to true wisdom and understanding will promote peace in the community. And according to James, righteousness is "sown in peace by those who make peace" (v. 18). If we desire to see a "harvest of righteousness," it is achieved through a commitment to peace. Yeshua said, "Blessed are the peacemakers, for they shall be called sons of God" (Matthew 5:9). Ultimately God is the source of true peace; thus,

---

3 David Nystrom, The NIV Application Commentary: James (Grand Rapids, MI: Zondervan, 1997). EPUB: James 3:13-18, para. 22

those who pursue peace are called His sons because they take after their Father.

Living Wisely

The Bible warns against not only sinful behavior but also foolish behavior. It encourages us to be not only holy but also wise. Literally hundreds of verses in the Bible are devoted to this topic. But what is wisdom, and why is it so important?

Charles Spurgeon defines wisdom as "the right use of knowledge."[4] That is to say, merely possessing knowledge and understanding does not mean you have wisdom. Wisdom is the ability to make good judgments and rightly *apply* knowledge and understanding. Theologically speaking, wisdom comes from God (Proverbs 2:6). Moreover, wisdom from God is embodied in the Messiah (1 Corinthians 1:30). Thus, living wisely is a means by which we reflect the image and character of the Messiah to the world.

Living wisely is about navigating the world God created according to God's revealed truth. It is how we experience blessing and success in life. Due to the nature of our fallen world, living wisely is certainly not a guarantee against pain and suffering, as we can clearly see in Job and Ecclesiastes. Nevertheless, as we see in the book of Proverbs, we can generally expect good results when we apply wise principles.

Indeed, wisdom is a necessary component to being a disciple of Yeshua. And it's necessary for experiencing blessing and success as we navigate this life. But how do we become wise? The Bible tells us a number of ways.

---

4 Charles H. Spurgeon, *A Sermon No. 991* (Metropolitan Tabernacle, Newington, 4/27/1871).

First, we must acknowledge the source of true wisdom: "For the Lord gives wisdom; from his mouth come knowledge and understanding" (Proverbs 2:6). While an earthly wisdom can be gained apart from God, this is a counterfeit wisdom. Earthly wisdom does not glorify God or produce blessing. It is built upon bitter jealousy and selfish ambition and results in "disorder and every vile practice" (James 3:14-16). True wisdom from God is built upon a "fear of the Lord" (Proverbs 1:7) and results in "a harvest of righteousness" (James 3:18).

Second, after we recognize that true wisdom comes from God, we must ask Him for it: "If any of you lacks wisdom, let him ask God, who gives generously to all without reproach, and it will be given him" (James 1:5). Our daily prayer upon waking up each morning ought to be, "God, give me wisdom to navigate life today for your glory." God gives generously to all who ask for wisdom and who commit to walk in what He has revealed to them.

Third, we gain wisdom by studying the Torah: "The law of the Lord is perfect, reviving the soul; the testimony of the Lord is sure, making wise the simple" (Psalm 19:7). When we meditate on God's Word, the psalmist says we become "like a tree planted by streams of water that yields its fruit in its season, and its leaf does not wither" (Psalm 1:3). God has generously revealed His vast wisdom to us in the written Scriptures. If we want to glean from God's wisdom, all we need to do is pick up the Bible and read it.

Fourth, we gain wisdom by walking with those who are wise: "Whoever walks with the wise becomes wise, but the companion of fools will suffer harm" (Proverbs 13:20). When we spend time with wise teachers—listening to them, observing how they act, learning from them—we become wise ourselves. And if this is true of wise people on earth today, how much more is it true of our Messiah? We ought to be walking with our Messiah daily, observing how He acted and learning from His teachings in the Scriptures. The Messiah embodies wisdom according to Scripture. Therefore, becoming like our Messiah helps us to become more wise by default.

Fifth, we must spend time thinking about our death: "So teach us to number our days that we may get a heart of wisdom" (Psalm 90:12). Solomon said that the heart of the wise is in the "house of mourning" (Ecclesiastes 7:4). Thinking about death is not easy or fun. It's sorrowful and often painful. Nevertheless, it's good for our soul. When we consider how short this life really is, it helps us get our priorities straight. We begin to live more wisely. We stop wasting time on the things that don't matter and we start appreciating the things that do matter.

So let us pursue wisdom! "How much better to get wisdom than gold! To get understanding is to be chosen rather than silver" (Proverbs 16:16). Living wisely not only brings glory to God but also helps us live a happier and more fulfilled life.

CHAPTER 13

DRAW NEAR TO GOD

What causes quarrels and what causes fights among you? Is it not this, that your passions are at war within you? You desire and do not have, so you murder. You covet and cannot obtain, so you fight and quarrel. You do not have, because you do not ask. You ask and do not receive, because you ask wrongly, to spend it on your passions. You adulterous people! Do you not know that friendship with the world is enmity with God? Therefore whoever wishes to be a friend of the world makes himself an enemy of God. Or do you suppose it is to no purpose that the Scripture says, "He yearns jealously over the spirit that he has made to dwell in us"? But he gives more grace. Therefore it says, "God opposes the proud but gives grace to the humble." Submit yourselves therefore to God. Resist the devil, and he will flee from you. Draw near to God, and he will draw near to you. Cleanse your hands, you sinners, and purify your hearts, you double-minded. Be wretched and mourn and weep. Let your laughter be turned to mourning and your joy to gloom. Humble yourselves before the Lord, and he will exalt you.

James 4:1-10

This section of James' epistle continues to build upon the themes introduced in the previous chapter. James said, "Where jealousy and selfish ambition exist, there will be disorder and every vile practice" (3:16). We now see that this disorder and vile practice, rooted in jealousy and selfish ambition, often takes the form of quarrels and fighting within the congregation. James asks, "What causes quarrels and what causes fights among you?" He follows that with another question that reveals the answer: "Is it not this, that your passions are at war within you?" In other words, we are at war with everyone else because we're at war within ourselves. Paul likewise wrote that we are fighting an inward war between the desire to live a holy life for God and the carnal desire to continue in sin

(Romans 7:7-25). "Passions" is translated from the Greek word *hedone*, from which we get the word *hedonism*. Hedonism is "the doctrine that pleasure or happiness is the sole or chief good in life."[1] Indeed, strife and hostility in our relationships are ultimately birthed from our inward desires for personal power, position, fame, etc., above all else. These inward passions result in running over anyone who gets in the way.

James said, "You desire and do not have, so you murder" (v. 2). Once again, James echoes Yeshua's Sermon on the Mount, showing that murder is deeper than literally killing a person; it's a condition of the heart expressed outwardly in anger. However, scholars do suggest that "murder" could actually be taken literally in some sense. Keener writes:

> Teachers often used hyperbole: graphic, rhetorical exaggeration for effect. Presumably most members of James's original audience had never literally killed anyone, but they were exposed to violent teachers (3:13-18) who regarded killing as a satisfactory means of attaining justice and redistribution of wealth. Or James may think of wealthy landowners ready to kill others to achieve their ends.[2]

In either case, murder is connected here to covetousness—an inward desire of the heart. James teaches us that sin originates from our heart's desires (1:15). Therefore, even if the "murder" James condemns here is meant figuratively, we can see how such anger

---

1 "hedonism." *Merriam-Webster*. www.merriam-webster.com. Accessed 12/5/18

2 Craig Keener, *NIV Cultural Backgrounds Study Bible: Bringing to Life the Ancient World of Scripture*, James 4:2 (Grand Rapids, MI: Zondervan, 2016)

within the heart could lead to literal murder. In fact, the Didache, a first century Christian treatise, states just that:

> Be not prone to anger, for anger leads to murder; nor be zealous, contentious, or irascible. For from all these are born acts of murder. (Didache 3:2-3)[3]

James now moves on to the topic of denied prayer requests. He says, "You ask and do not receive, because you ask wrongly, to spend it on your passions" (v. 3). In other words, God doesn't give you what you've asked for because your motivation is merely to spend it on your own selfish ambitions. God is not going to honor self-centered requests that ultimately bring harm to the community. McKnight writes:

> Their prayers, instead of being directed at gaining wisdom, explored and sought to increase their own consuming zeal and ambition for power. Wise church leaders know the fine line between wanting what God wants and wanting what they want; the teachers in James's community had erased that line and were now well beyond it.[4]

Throughout the Scriptures, the image of adultery is often applied to idolatry and unfaithfulness to God's commandments (Hosea 3:1; Jeremiah 3:6-20). That's why James calls out his readers for their adultery: "You adulterous people! Do you not know that friendship with

---

3 Bart. D. Ehrman, *The Apostolic Fathers Vol. 1* (Cambridge, MA: Harvard University Press, 2003), p. 421

4 Scot McKnight, *The New International Commentary of the New Testament: The Letter of James* (Grand Rapids, MI: Wm. B. Eerdmans Publishing Co., 2011) pp. 330-331

the world is enmity with God? Therefore whoever wishes to be a friend of the world makes himself an enemy of God" (v. 4). James saw covetousness as a form of idolatry. Paul makes the same observation: "Put to death therefore what is earthly in you: sexual immorality, impurity, passion, evil desire, and covetousness, which is idolatry" (Colossians 3:5). James continues to expound on the dichotomy he set up toward the beginning of his epistle between our own selfish agendas, which bring forth death and disorder, and the wisdom and purpose we receive from God, which bring forth life and peace. As James says, you cannot be a faithful follower of Messiah and a friend of the world at the same time. It's a divided allegiance.

James 4:5 is notoriously ambiguous, and apparently scholars have sharp disagreements regarding how it ought to be interpreted and translated. For instance, what scripture is James referencing? Nothing in the Tanakh matches James' statement, "He yearns jealously over the spirit that he has made to dwell in us." Nystrom[5] suggests that James is perhaps loosely paraphrasing a passage like Exodus 34:14: "For you shall worship no other god, for the Lord, whose name is Jealous, is a jealous God." McKnight argues that James is referring to Proverbs 3:34, which is quoted in the sixth verse: "James is referring to Proverbs 3:34, which he will cite in the next verse but suspends from view until he has clarified himself so that the text will make more sense."[6] Still other scholars, like Richard Bauckham, suggest that James is quoting an extra-biblical source: "Verse 4:5 probably quotes a no

5 David Nystrom, *The NIV Application Commentary: James* (Grand Rapids, MI: Zondervan, 1997). EPUB: James 4:1-10, para 21

6 Scot McKnight, *The New International Commentary of the New Testament: The Letter of James* (Grand Rapids, MI: Wm. B. Eerdmans Publishing Co., 2011) p. 336

longer extant apocryphal work."[7] In either case, James' point is that God greatly yearns for His people to be faithful and to look to Him for wisdom instead of turning to the world.

While James certainly issues a stinging rebuke against those who are stirring up strife within the community, he reassures them that forgiveness is available. All they need to do is humble themselves and repent: "But he gives more grace. Therefore it says, 'God opposes the proud but gives grace to the humble'" (v. 6). James unpacks what it really means to humble yourself and repent in the verses that follow.

First, we are told, "Submit yourselves therefore to God" (v. 7). This means recognizing that you previously haven't been in submission to God. You've been a slave to your own passions. As Yeshua said, we cannot serve two masters. Thus, turn away from your own passions and submit to God.

Second, "Resist the devil, and he will flee from you" (v. 7). Recognize that Satan is actively trying to intimidate and deceive you. Walking in submission to God means standing up against the schemes of the enemy. The apostle Peter echoes the imperative to resist the devil: "Be sober-minded; be watchful. Your adversary the devil prowls around like a roaring lion, seeking someone to devour. Resist him, firm in your faith, knowing that the same kinds of suffering are being experienced by your brotherhood throughout the world" (1 Peter 5:8-9).

Third, "Draw near to God, and he will draw near to you" (v. 8). Accept God's invitation of fellowship. Take that step toward God and His divine presence will meet you at that step. James here is using

---

7 Richard Bauckham, *New Testament Readings: James* (New York, NY: Taylor & Francis e-Library, 2002), p. 217

the Temple service as a metaphor. Interestingly, the Hebrew word for "offering" is *korban*, which has its root in the verb *karav*, meaning "to draw near." When a worshipper would bring an offering to the Temple, they were "drawing near" to God.

Fourth, drawing near to God is connected to cleansed hands and a pure heart: "Cleanse your hands, you sinners, and purify your hearts, you double-minded" (v. 8). This, again, draws upon the Temple service, specifically the priestly purification rites, as a metaphor for spiritual cleansing. Repentance and walking in submission to God require both inward and outward change—faith that produces good works.

Fifth, "Be wretched and mourn and weep. Let your laughter be turned to mourning and your joy to gloom" (v. 9). True repentance, according to James, requires being filled with deep remorse and guilt. Too often sin is treated as a light matter and even laughed at. True humility and repentance acknowledges the sheer weight of sin. David's prayer of repentance after the Bathsheba incident comes to mind: "The sacrifices of God are a broken spirit; a broken and contrite heart, O God, you will not despise" (Psalm 51:17). McKee notes that this verse "includes some of the themes of Yom Kippur or the Day of Atonement, where God's people are to be focused on their sins and shortcomings, be widely unhappy, and repent of their errors from the previous year."[8]

James wraps up his series of admonitions with this: "Humble yourselves before the Lord, and he will exalt you" (v. 10). Striving for power and position for selfish reasons ends only in disorder and chaos. Submitting to your passions will not give you what you truly want.

---

8 J.K. McKee, *James for the Practical Messianic* (Richardson, TX: Messianic Apologetics, 2013), p. 114

True peace, love, and joy are found only in a right relationship with God, which is achieved through humility and repentance. As Yeshua said, "Whoever exalts himself will be humbled, and whoever humbles himself will be exalted" (Matthew 23:12).

Is There Emptiness in Your Life?

Many of us carry around a deep sense of rejection, insecurity, and longing. We struggle to feel accepted and valued, which can often drive us to unhealthy behavior. We obsess over relationships or careers or positions within our community because we find our value and security in those things. Anything or anyone that might come in between us and our passions is a serious threat—we struggle and fight and strive to hold on to our source of value and security.

Jacob lived a life of constant struggle. Even while he was still in his mother's womb, he struggled with his brother Esau (Genesis 25:22). When he was born, he came out holding Esau's heel, foreshadowing his desire to be the firstborn. Jacob's name, *Ya'akov*, literally means "to grab the heel." His name and reputation later came to be associated with deception (Genesis 27:36).

Jacob's constant striving to get ahead, even to the point of deceiving and manipulating people to get what he wanted, got him in all kinds of trouble. His antics led to his brother Esau vowing to kill him (Genesis 27:36). It led to his family breaking up. How did this character deficiency develop and take over within Jacob? You might say Jacob's treatment by his parents influenced his behavior:

> Isaac loved Esau because he ate of his game, but Rebekah loved Jacob. (Genesis 25:28)

It seems that parental favoritism was at play in the family. The father preferred Esau while the mother preferred Jacob. Perhaps Jacob wanted to be the firstborn because, like all young boys, he longed for the love and affection of his father. He might have thought, "If I could just be like Esau, my father will love me." Perhaps this played a small part in his decision to disguise himself as Esau in order to receive a blessing from his father. Unfavored children often grow up with the constant need to feel validated, which is ultimately fueled by a deep sense of rejection. A parent's love and presence are key to a child's emotional and spiritual health.

Whether it's because of a lack of acceptance from our parents or some other reason, many of us can relate to Jacob. We have grown up with feelings of rejection, which have often led us to try to find acceptance, security, and an identity in the wrong places. The tragic thing about Jacob's efforts is that, while he was able to swindle his brother out of his birthright and steal the blessing by deceiving his father, he reaped the rotten fruit of those choices. He thought that getting the birthright and the blessing would finally fill up his emptiness. But all it did was cause strife and disorder within his family and leave him unsatisfied.

Likewise, we often think that achieving some level of earthly status in life will bring us fulfillment. We find our identity in climbing the corporate ladder, obtaining some position within our church or community, getting that relationship, job, or house that we want. Sometimes we even use less-than-honest means to accomplish our selfish ambitions. Like Jacob, we hurt others in our drive for success. Much of our striving is simply an attempt to find some sort of relief from our pain, but our inner emptiness isn't satisfied even when we finally get what we've been striving for.

The turning point in Jacob's life was not when he successfully stole the blessing. It wasn't when he got married. It wasn't when he attained tremendous wealth and success. It was when he had a transformative encounter with God. Jacob found the true source of blessing when He allowed God to define his identity. He wrestled with God, and it was declared, "Your name shall no longer be called Jacob, but Israel" (Genesis 32:28). He was no longer to be known by his former reputation of deception or his longing to be the firstborn of his father, Isaac. He was now defined as an accepted and loved "firstborn son" (Exodus 4:22) of his heavenly Father.

Likewise, our inner emptiness can be satisfied only by looking to God. Our earthly fathers might have failed to give us what we needed, and we might suffer from a desperate need to feel special, but we can find healing and acceptance in the presence of our heavenly Father. Even if we've brought strife and disorder to our families and communities through our selfish ambition, God's grace is available to us when we repent:

> Humble yourselves before the Lord, and he will exalt you.
> (James 4:10)

Our heavenly Father is the one who blesses us and gives us purpose and identity. And from that basis we can be freed from the chains of our own passions at war within us. We no longer need to strive, manipulate, or run people over in a desperate attempt to feel valuable and accepted. When we allow God to define our identity as His child, He gives us new desires—a hunger and thirst for righteousness—which He promises to satisfy (Matthew 5:6).

Living in CommUNITY

From the very beginning, we see that God's divine purpose for man includes being in community. Indeed, God Himself said, "It is not good that man should be alone" (Genesis 2:18). God declared everything else in creation *tov* (good), but He apparently thought it was a problem that Adam didn't have any fellowship. So what did He do? He established the very first community of believers by creating Eve, thus showing that God's divine will for man is perfected in the fellowship and unity of His people.

But why is community so important to God? For one thing, John says we cannot love God if we do not love our brothers and sisters in the faith (1 John 4:20). How can we truly love our brothers and sisters if we aren't in fellowship with any of them? Furthermore, biblical community is the means by which God fulfills His will on earth. When we become disciples of Yeshua, we become part of the body of Messiah. All members need to be available and working for the body to fulfill its role (1 Corinthians 12:14-27). Living isolated from other believers has no biblical framework. In fact, the Bible explicitly discourages it:

> Whoever isolates himself seeks his own desire; he breaks out against all sound judgment. (Proverbs 18:1)

Believers generally agree with the need for fellowship, so the problem isn't really a lack of God-given desire for community. The problem is that many believers don't know how to maintain unity when they find fellowship. Just like it was in the first century, there are quarrels, fights, and divisions among us (vv. 1-4). This is deeply alarming. Why? Because Yeshua said that the world would know the Father sent Him when His followers are united (John 17:21). Therefore, disunity in the congregation is a detriment to the Gospel.

Thankfully, the Bible gives us several keys for having unity in the body for God's glory.

The first key to having biblical unity is humility. We know this because the antithesis of humility—pride—is the number one hindrance to unity. Pride is the first of seven deadly sins that God hates. From pride come wicked and murderous intentions, lies, gossip, and ultimately "discord among brothers" (Proverbs 6:16-19). On the other side, Ephesians 4:2-3 says that those eager to maintain unity of the Spirit do so with humility, gentleness, and patience.

Everything starts with humility. We can't even come to the Messiah in repentance if we aren't humble enough to acknowledge that we need Him. James says that God gives grace to the humble but opposes the proud (v. 6). In addition, Yeshua says that being great in the Kingdom requires us to humble ourselves by serving others:

> "But whoever would be great among you must be your servant, and whoever would be first among you must be your slave, even as the Son of Man came not to be served but to serve, and to give His life as a ransom for many." (Matthew 20:26-28)

Our Messiah Yeshua demonstrated this biblical characteristic in an amazing way when He washed the feet of His disciples (John 13:1-17). In the first century, this task was reserved for the lowest of servants. When Yeshua performed this act of humility, He was showing us how we should serve one another: "For I have given you an example, that you also should do just as I have done to you" (John 13:15). Are you willing to humble yourself and serve others in your community?

The second key is accountability—that is, the willingness to be honest and accept responsibility. James says that we are to confess our sins to one another (5:16). We're awfully good at making excuses and finding ways to avoid following this instruction. Some of us are so guarded because of past hurts that we aren't willing to let ourselves be vulnerable. But accountability is key to the unity of the body. In fact, when God speaks, it is often through other people. If we aren't willing to humble ourselves and trust others enough to be vulnerable with them, we often shut the door to what God wants to speak into our lives.

In addition to being held accountable, we must be willing to hold others accountable. That's what community is for. Sometimes being confronted by other believers is uncomfortable, especially when it's in regard to sin. It's also uncomfortable to be the one doing the confronting! But for the sake of the Kingdom, we need to get over our pride and fear in this area. Paul says, "Brothers, if anyone is caught in any transgression, you who are spiritual should restore him in a spirit of gentleness. Keep watch on yourself, lest you too be tempted. Bear one another's burdens, and so fulfill the law of Christ" (Galatians 6:1-2).

The third key is generosity. The Torah tells us to meet the needs of our brothers and sisters in the community (Deuteronomy 15:7-11). That may seem simple enough, but we need to remember that poverty is not only a physical condition. It's possible for someone to be emotionally poor, too. Often many people in the community are depressed and in desperate need of encouragement. How generous are you? How much time do you invest in listening to those in your faith community? How often do you look for opportunities to speak into someone's life? How much time per week do you spend serving others? As believers, we need to be generous with our words, time, and finances. We need to always be on the lookout for ways to bless our brothers and sisters in the community concerning both their physical and emotional needs.

The fourth key to having unity in the body is tradition. Sadly, tradition has been given a bad rap by some believers. While Yeshua explicitly condemns certain traditions that replace or otherwise go against God's commandments, He practiced and taught many other traditions. Traditions help us stay connected to our heritage. They remind us who we are. They give us common ground with each other.

The Jewish people are a wonderful example of the power of tradition. In addition to God's amazing love and faithfulness to the Jewish people, tradition is what helped the Jewish people stay united as a nation for thousands of years. In fact, the feast days of God (Leviticus 23)—His "traditions," if you will—are designed for the very purpose of bringing all Israel together several times a year. Is it possible that the disunity in the body that we see today is partly due to Christianity disconnecting from its Jewish roots and throwing out God's "traditions"?

The fifth and most important key to unity within the body of Messiah is the Messiah Himself. When our focus as a community is on Yeshua rather than our own agendas, we become conformed to His image and character and grow in love for each other. Only then can we truly be on the same page in mind and spirit:

> May the God of endurance and encouragement grant you to live in such harmony with one another, in accord with Christ Jesus, that together you may with one voice glorify the God and Father of our Lord Jesus Christ. (Romans 15:5-6)

Indeed, selfish ambition and personal pride bring disorder, strife, and division (James 3:16). A community of believers may have minor theological differences, but the Messiah must remain central for the community to survive and flourish. Yeshua said that a house built on sand cannot stand, but the house built on the rock will not fall when the rain and winds come (Matthew 7:24-27). May the Father unite His people upon the rock!

CHAPTER 14

DO NOT JUDGE

Do not speak evil against one another, brothers. The one who speaks against a brother or judges his brother, speaks evil against the law and judges the law. But if you judge the law, you are not a doer of the law but a judge. There is only one lawgiver and judge, he who is able to save and to destroy. But who are you to judge your neighbor?
James 4:11-12

James begins this section of his epistle with a command: "Do not speak evil against one another, brothers" (v. 11). Evil speech was evidently part of the quarrels and fights mentioned earlier in this chapter (4:1-4). James' command here goes back to his previous statements about controlling your speech. That is, faith in Yeshua is incompatible with evil speech (3:10-12). And if you cannot stop yourself from speaking evil against your neighbor, your religion is worthless (1:26).

"Speak evil" is translated from the Greek, *katalaleo*. According to McKnight, "The sense of the term here is speaking accusingly, falsely, degradingly, dishonorably, and with libelous or slanderous intent in order to label a person as dangerous or unworthy."[1] This type of speech is utterly hostile and belittling. Of course, we know that speaking evil against your brother or sister is a direct violation of the Torah (Leviticus 19:16) and also consistently condemned throughout the Tanakh (Psalm 50:20-22; 101:5; Proverbs 10:18; 26:22-24). Ultimately, as James said previously, speaking evil against someone is a failure to hon-

1 Scot McKnight, *The New International Commentary of the New Testament: The Letter of James* (Grand Rapids, MI: Wm. B. Eerdmans Publishing Co., 2011) p. 361

or them as a creature made in God's image (3:9) and, therefore, is a failure to honor God.

James connects speaking evil with judging: "The one who speaks against a brother or judges his brother, speaks evil against the law and judges the law" (v. 11). Obviously James does not prohibit all forms of judging—throughout his own epistle he makes some pretty severe judgments! He strongly affirms discerning right from wrong and lovingly bringing correction. The type of judging James prohibits is condemnation. We don't have the right to condemn anyone.

James' argument can be summed up as follows: Speaking against and judging your brother is to speak against and judge the Torah. How? The Torah commands us not to speak evil against our brother. Thus, by rejecting the Torah's command, we elevate ourselves above the Torah as a judge, essentially declaring that the Torah is faulty in its condemnation of evil speech and that our ways are superior: "But if you judge the law, you are not a doer of the law but a judge" (v. 11). Only God has the authority to define right and wrong and to judge (condemn): "There is only one lawgiver and judge, he who is able to save and to destroy" (v. 12). So who do we think we are to attempt to hijack God's position?

Who Are You to Judge?

It is often said that believers ought not to judge. Indeed, "Judge not that you be not judged" (Matthew 7:1) is one of the most memorized Bible verses of all time. Even people who have never read a Bible in their life will quote that verse to silence anyone who might dare express disapproval toward their lifestyle. But are we truly not to ever judge anyone?

The idea that it's wrong to judge at all has two problems. First, it's self-defeating. If it's wrong to judge, you would never be able to say that it's wrong. You can't say that someone is wrong for judging because you would be judging them. You would be wrong for saying that they're wrong!

Second, the Bible explicitly commands us to judge. For instance, the Lord commanded the judges of Israel to hear each case and to render just judgments (e.g. Deuteronomy 1:16). This was a serious job. In some cases, people's lives were at stake. Thus, the judges needed to be careful, discerning, and fair in delivering their rulings. Yeshua taught His followers these same principles: "Do not judge by mere appearances, but judge with right judgment" (John 7:24). Just like the judges of Israel, we all must be careful, discerning, and fair in our judgments. That means, for example, hearing all the evidence (Proverbs 18:13) and not immediately jumping to conclusions about people and situations on the basis of hearsay or incomplete information.

If Yeshua didn't prohibit judging—and indeed commanded it—what do we make of Yeshua's statement in Matthew 7:1? What did He mean when He said, "Judge not that you be not judged"? The parallel passage in Luke's gospel gives us some insight:

> "Judge not, and you will not be judged; *condemn not, and you will not be condemned*; forgive, and you will be forgiven." (Luke 6:37, emphasis added)

Here we see that the type of judging Yeshua forbids is condemnation. It is not our place to condemn; only God has that authority. As James says, "There is only one lawgiver and judge, he who is able to save and to destroy. But who are you to judge your neighbor?" (v. 12) The danger of condemning our neighbor and thus hijacking God's position as judge is that He will judge us in accordance with how we've judged others: "For with the judgment you pronounce you will be judged, and with the measure you use it will be measured to you" (Matthew 7:2). Tim Hegg writes:

> It is with God as the final and ultimate judge in mind that the opening phrase should be understood. He teaches us that we dare not usurp the place of God as Judge, for if we do, we will answer to Him. We might paraphrase: "Do not usurp the place of God as judge so that you will not be judged yourself by God."[2]

So far we've learned that judging with right judgment entails being fair, discerning, and hearing all the evidence rather than jumping to conclusions. Also, a license to judge is not a license to condemn! In fact, a righteous judge must be willing to extend mercy. When a sinner presents genuine humility and repentance, God forgives them. Since God is the perfect judge, we ought to look to His example in this area and thus be willing to forgive. Just as God judges us on the basis of our judgment toward others, He will forgive us on the basis of our forgiveness toward others (Matthew 6:12). Therefore, it's incumbent upon us to show mercy toward repentant sinners just as we've been shown mercy.

Another aspect of right judgment is that it is without hypocrisy. For example, nobody wants to listen to a serial adulterer give marriage advice. Thus, we shouldn't judge others if we are unwilling to judge ourselves first. We need to be humble and acknowledge our own sin

---

2 Tim Hegg, *Commentary on the Gospel of Matthew Chapters 1-7* (Tacoma, WA: TorahResource, 2007) p. 263

and need for forgiveness before we talk to others about their sins. This is clear as we continue reading Yeshua's teaching on judging:

> "Why do you see the speck that is in your brother's eye, but do not notice the log that is in your own eye? Or how can you say to your brother, 'Let me take the speck out of your eye,' when there is the log in your own eye? You hypocrite, first take the log out of your own eye, and then you will see clearly to take the speck out of your brother's eye." (Matthew 7:3-5)

Notice that Yeshua didn't say not to take the speck out of your brother's eye. We should indeed humbly look after our neighbor in love and care for their spiritual wellbeing, correcting them when necessary, but only after we have carefully examined ourselves so that we are not guilty of hypocrisy. We should not only repent of our own sin before approaching our neighbor but also keep in mind that we share common ground. We've all sinned and fallen short of God's glory. It's not wrong to speak the truth, but we need to consider *how* we speak the truth. The truth is more willingly received when it is presented with humility and empathy.

In summary, you need to ask yourself these questions: Are you careful, discerning, and fair? Do you take the time to hear all the evidence before drawing a conclusion? Are you willing to extend mercy? Have you repented of your own sins, and do you approach others on the common ground that we're all in need of grace? We all make judgments. Let's make sure we're making right judgments.

CHAPTER 15

SUBMIT TO GOD'S WILL

Come now, you who say, "Today or tomorrow we will go into such and such a town and spend a year there and trade and make a profit"—yet you do not know what tomorrow will bring. What is your life? For you are a mist that appears for a little time and then vanishes. Instead you ought to say, "If the Lord wills, we will live and do this or that." As it is, you boast in your arrogance. All such boasting is evil. So whoever knows the right thing to do and fails to do it, for him it is sin.

James 4:13-17

In this passage, James condemns another form of evil speech: arrogant boasting. He targets merchants who make presumptuous claims about their future plans to travel and spend a year making money. Keener explains that people in the Roman Empire acquired wealth in two main ways: being a landowner or a merchant.[1] James addresses merchants in this passage and wealthy landowners in the next chapter.

Obviously, James is not against making plans or acquiring wealth. He is simply using this as an outline to set up his argument against arrogant boasting, which is clear in the verses that follow: "Yet you do not know what tomorrow will bring. What is your life? For you are a mist that appears for a little time and then vanishes" (v. 14). Again, what James condemns here is not the merchants' planning or desire to make wealth but their presumptuous attitude—acting as though they, not God, are in control of their destiny.

---

1 Craig Keener, *NIV Cultural Backgrounds Study Bible: Bringing to Life the Ancient World of Scripture*, James 4:13-17 (Grand Rapids, MI: Zondervan, 2016)

James counters this arrogant boasting by reminding us that the future is uncertain. As the proverb says, "Do not boast about tomorrow, for you do not know what a day may bring" (Proverbs 27:1). Therefore, to trust solely in our own plans is foolish. Everything that we've built can come crumbling down tomorrow. Like a mist, the life we've built can disappear in an instant. To exalt ourselves in our plans as if the future is certain and God is out of the picture is not only foolish but also evil. We ought to humbly bring our plans before God and ask for God's direction and blessing. In fact, failing to go to God is sin, according to James: "So whoever knows the right thing to do and fails to do it, for him it is sin" (v. 17). As Nystrom puts it, "The making of plans as though the future is certain is itself a sin, because functionally it is a denial of God, either his importance or even his very existence. Then to boast about it is a further sin."[2]

James is essentially attacking the foolish idea that God is not sovereign over your life. His point is not that you shouldn't plan ahead or that you need to ritualistically declare, "If the Lord wills," every time you make even the smallest decision. His point is that your life is not yours. We need to be humble and ask ourselves what is really fueling our lives and our plans. Is God at the center of your business, your ministry, your home? Are your plans made in light of living for His glory and His ultimate purposes or yours?

Are You Following God's Will or Your Own?

Being a follower of Yeshua is to deny yourself and surrender your life to the will of God (Luke 9:23). The Messiah is not just some accessory that you've added to your life; He *is* your life. And everything

---

2 David Nystrom, The NIV Application Commentary: James (Grand Rapids, MI: Zondervan, 1997). EPUB: James 4:11-17, para 25

you do—your ministry, your work, etc.—is to be done for His glory and according to His will. As John MacArthur once said, "Nothing is more characteristic of a Christian than a desire to do the will of God."[3]

While most Christians would agree that we are to do God's will, it's easy to fall into the trap of mistaking God's will for our own. Or to put it another way, *using* "God's will" as a means to an end—that is, dressing up our selfish ambition in religious clothes and calling it "God's will." This deception is especially dangerous because it gives us a false sense of security. We feel that our selfish ambition is religiously justified because we're "doing the will of God." But in reality, we're using God to do our own will.

For instance, God commands us to rest on the Sabbath. Some Messianics and other Torah observant Christians might use this command as an excuse not to attend church on the Sabbath. They'll say, "I just don't feel like I'm able to rest by coming to church." This is a great example of having a sense of religious justification in going against God's will. God's will for us is not only to rest on the Sabbath but also to have a holy gathering with other believers (Leviticus 23:3). We justify our neglect to meet with our community on the Sabbath by thinking we're observing the command to rest. In reality, we're lazy and don't feel like leaving the house. Thus, we aren't really keeping the Sabbath for God's glory and according to His will. We "keep" it in accordance with our own selfish desires.

Ministers ought to especially be on guard against this deception. Leaders in ministry are often tempted to make up religious excuses for taking unwise risks—financial and otherwise—in attempts

3 John MacArthur, *Grace to You*. "Responding to the Will of God." www.gty.org. Accessed 8/5/18

to grow their ministries. Unneeded and expensive assets are often hastily purchased with God's money, putting financial strain on the ministry or Church community. In addition, many "Bible teachers," particularly those with an online platform, will give messages on sensational and borderline conspiratorial topics based on highly speculative and dubious information. Even if they have doubts about much of the information themselves, they justify their teachings on those topics with excuses such as, "A lot of people will watch this sermon on YouTube due to the nature of the content—thus more views, subscribers, and potential donors! The ministry will grow and we'll be able to reach more people!" Taking unwise risks and knowingly feeding God's sheep theological junk food, even if the goal is to grow and supposedly reach more people, is evidence of a divided allegiance to Yeshua. But the selfish ambition is extremely difficult to detect when it's wrapped up in so many religious excuses.

We all have a desire for comfort and happiness. We all have goals and ambitions. These things are not wrong in themselves, but our human nature struggles to pursue them in light of God's authority over our lives. We all want to live our life on our own terms, putting God in second place to our goals and desires—and that's what makes them idols.

This struggle obviously doesn't go away when we make the commitment to follow the Messiah. We just find ways to delude ourselves into thinking that our motives aren't actually selfish. As blogger Timothy Dalrymple so eloquently puts it:

> We hitch our own personal and professional ambitions to the purposes of the Almighty, convincing ourselves that pursuing them is simply the response of an obedient servant. We tell ourselves we are "called" in ways that just happen to gratify our

> ego and/or advance our material comforts and power. This is what using religion for ourselves means.[4]

Followers of Messiah need to make sure we are not using religion for ourselves. We have to make the decision daily to surrender our own will to God. We need to examine our hearts and sincerely ask God to expose how we haven't been living in accordance with His will, and perhaps even some of the ways we've religiously justified ourselves in our disobedience. And then we need to pray that God would put us back into spiritual alignment so that we can truly have lasting fulfillment, which can be found only when we are living in His will.

4 Timothy Dalrymple, *Patheos*. "Mistaking God's Will for Our Own." www.patheos.com. Accessed 12/16/18

CHAPTER 16

SPEAK OUT AGAINST INJUSTICE

Come now, you rich, weep and howl for the miseries that are coming upon you. Your riches have rotted and your garments are moth-eaten. Your gold and silver have corroded, and their corrosion will be evidence against you and will eat your flesh like fire. You have laid up treasure in the last days. Behold, the wages of the laborers who mowed your fields, which you kept back by fraud, are crying out against you, and the cries of the harvesters have reached the ears of the Lord of hosts. You have lived on the earth in luxury and in self-indulgence. You have fattened your hearts in a day of slaughter. You have condemned and murdered the righteous person. He does not resist you.

James 5:1-6

James now turns his attention to wealthy landowners who have been oppressing their workers. He issues a prophetic warning of calamity and destruction against the "rich." As I've already noted, James is not against acquiring wealth or being rich. God can certainly permit and direct a life of wealth, as we see with Abraham, King David, and many others. Moreover, Joseph of Arimathea, who played a key role in Yeshua's burial after His crucifixion, was a rich man who is identified as a disciple of Yeshua (Matthew 27:57). According to McKnight, "James uses the language 'rich people' very much the way Jesus did: it is 'code' for the oppressors of the messianic community."[1] To James, wealth itself is not the problem. The problem is gaining wealth in unjust ways—through oppression and exploitation. Living a

---

1 Scot McKnight, *The New International Commentary of the New Testament: The Letter of James* (Grand Rapids, MI: Wm. B. Eerdmans Publishing Co., 2011) p. 383

life of excessive luxury while expressing indifference toward the poor is likewise condemned.

Similar to Yeshua's teaching (Matthew 6:20), James reminds his readers that their wealth here on earth will not last forever. The moths and rust will take it from them in the end: "Your riches have rotted and your garments are moth-eaten. Your gold and silver have corroded" (vv. 2-3) In fact, all their corroded wealth that they've hoarded will be "evidence" against them on the day of judgment—testifying to their guilt and ultimately destroying them: "...and will eat your flesh like fire" (v. 3).

Just as the blood of the murdered Abel "cried out" against Cain (Genesis 4:10), the withheld wages of the defrauded laborers cry out against the wealthy landowners. In the first century, laborers who worked for these landowners were paid by the day, and they relied on their daily wages to provide for their families. To hold back their wages was essentially to rob them. These landowners were in explicit violation of the Torah:

> You shall not oppress a hired worker who is poor and needy, whether he is one of your brothers or one of the sojourners who are in your land within your towns. You shall give him his wages on the same day, before the sun sets (for he is poor and counts on it), lest he cry against you to the Lord, and you be guilty of sin. (Deuteronomy 24:14-15)

The sin of the rich reaches its climax in verse 6: "You have condemned and murdered the righteous person." Keener observes that landlords sometimes literally killed their tenants: "A few landowners even had their own hit squads of hired assassins to deal with uncooperative tenants."[2] Thus, one of the major problems of wealth worship is that it's all-consuming. It drives people to the point that they are willing to do anything to maintain power and control—even murder. McKnight points out that the phrase "you have condemned" is similar to what's in James 2:6-7, in which the rich are described as dragging the poor into court: "The language is from the courtroom; it describes abuse of power against the powerless with the intent to increase wealth and power."[3] The rich and powerful had the court system rigged in their favor and could abuse it to further oppress the poor.

James assures his oppressed readers that God has heard their cries. "The cries of the harvesters have reached the ears of the Lord of hosts" (v. 4). The wealthy landowners who have lived in excessive self-indulgence while oppressing the poor have been warned. Keener points out that James' prophetic warning "proved on the mark; a few years later the Judean aristocracy was mostly obliterated during the revolt against Rome."[4] With all the injustice that exists in our world today, James' words are more relevant now than ever. We can be assured that one day God will set everything right—the wicked oppressors will be condemned and the righteous oppressed will be delivered. We ought to look at how we treat others and sincerely consider whether we should be comforted or frightened by that reality.

---

2 Craig Keener, *NIV Cultural Backgrounds Study Bible: Bringing to Life the Ancient World of Scripture*, James: "Poverty and Revolt in Judea" (Grand Rapids, MI: Zondervan, 2016)

3 Scot McKnight, *The New International Commentary of the New Testament: The Letter of James* (Grand Rapids, MI: Wm. B. Eerdmans Publishing Co., 2011) p. 396

4 Craig Keener, *NIV Cultural Backgrounds Study Bible: Bringing to Life the Ancient World of Scripture*, James 5:1-6 (Grand Rapids, MI: Zondervan, 2016)

God's Justice: A Source of Hope

Many people today, including many Christians, struggle with the biblical teaching of God's justice. In our pluralistic society, it's unpopular to teach anything other than the idea that God accepts everyone and all behaviors. However, it's not our job craft a message that easily appeals to the secular world. Our job is to faithfully uphold what the Bible teaches, even when the message is unpopular. Nevertheless, the idea that God will one day execute judgment upon unrepentant sinners can certainly seem unpleasant, and it's meant to be. However, in a way it's also a source of hope.

First, why is it important that we recognize that God will punish the wicked? For one, it teaches us that the choices we make in this life matter. Our actions have consequences—*eternal* consequences. Goodness will be rewarded and wickedness will be punished. If our actions don't have consequences, then it really doesn't matter what anyone does. "Good" and "evil" would have no real meaning or value. If sin is not judged, then unrepentant rapists and child murderers just get away with the atrocities that they've committed. But if God is all-good (He is), then He cannot allow evil to go unpunished.

We can all understand this, because we all have a deep sense of justice and morality. Most people—even nonbelievers—yearn to see an end to oppression, violence, racism, sexual exploitation, etc. And although it often seems that things are hopeless and that evil is winning the day, we can have comfort in knowing that one day perfect justice will be enacted and evil will be abolished. While we have a responsibility to call out injustice and stand up for the rights of the oppressed in our world right now, we can breathe a sigh of relief that ultimate justice doesn't depend on us—God Himself will bring it about in His perfect timing. This is the hope expressed in the fifth chapter of James

(vv. 1-6)—the oppressors will one day face judgment and God's people will be delivered!

Furthermore, without God's judgment, God's mercy is meaningless. We all deserve God's wrath. We all deserve to be punished for the sins we've committed. But the good news is that we who've received the Messiah and have repented of our sins have been forgiven and redeemed. Salvation would mean nothing if there's nothing to be saved from. Thus, the reality of God's justice causes us to appreciate all the more the value of our salvation and the immense mercy of God toward us.

Everyone who cares about truth, morality, and justice ought to agree that God's judgment upon the wicked is important and necessary. Yeshua's death and resurrection offer forgiveness and hope to all who open their hearts to receive Him. But judgment and condemnation await those who reject Him and continue in their iniquity. This truth should energize us as believers to share the Gospel so that people know they have hope of salvation if they repent. And those who are walking in sin should be rightly frightened so that they heed the call to turn toward God. If the message of God's justice can offer us any comfort, it's that the same Messiah who died for us and gave us newness of life will also soon abolish all evil and suffering forever—bringing complete healing to our world.

CHAPTER 17

WAIT ON THE LORD

Be patient, therefore, brothers, until the coming of the Lord. See how the farmer waits for the precious fruit of the earth, being patient about it, until it receives the early and the late rains. You also, be patient. Establish your hearts, for the coming of the Lord is at hand. Do not grumble against one another, brothers, so that you may not be judged; behold, the Judge is standing at the door. As an example of suffering and patience, brothers, take the prophets who spoke in the name of the Lord. Behold, we consider those blessed who remained steadfast. You have heard of the steadfastness of Job, and you have seen the purpose of the Lord, how the Lord is compassionate and merciful. But above all, my brothers, do not swear, either by heaven or by earth or by an other oath, but let your "yes" be yes and your "no" be no, so that you may not fall under condemnation.

James 5:7-12

James now turns from the oppressors to the oppressed and offers them pastoral counsel on how they should respond in their difficult circumstances. As outlined in the previous section, James' readers can have hope that one day the Messiah will set everything right. God will execute His justice upon the wicked oppressors and deliver His people. In the meantime, however, they are to wait: "Be patient, therefore, brothers, until the coming of the Lord" (v. 7).

Why are we told to be patient and wait for the coming of the Lord? James gives the analogy of a farmer waiting for the "precious fruit of the earth" (v. 7). In other words, we don't wait for nothing. The farmer's toil and patience eventually leads to a wonderful, fruitful harvest. In the same way, we know that the coming of the Lord, which is "at hand," will make all the toil, struggling, and waiting more than worth it. In addition, as James taught earlier in his epistle, our patient endurance is key to our becoming "perfect and complete, lacking in nothing" (1:4). Therefore, James says, "Establish your hearts" (v. 8). We faithfully endure and count our trials as joy, knowing that God is refining our character and bringing us to spiritual maturity. And we're also strengthened by His promise of deliverance, which will soon come to pass.

In addition to exhorting us to have patient endurance as we await the coming of the Lord, James condemns another form of evil speech: complaining and grumbling. He says, "Do not grumble against one another, brothers, so that you may not be judged; behold, the Judge is standing at the door" (v. 9). Grumbling does nothing to bring relief to difficult circumstances—it only makes things worse! It takes everyone's eyes off the promise of God and stirs up fights and quarrels within the community. Not only that, but it incites the wrath of God, as we see throughout the Torah (e.g. Numbers 11:1).

James appeals to the prophets as an example of suffering and patience. He says that those who remained steadfast are considered blessed (v. 11). During His Sermon on the Mount, Yeshua likewise held the prophets up as an example to follow as we face persecution (Matthew 5:11-12). Just as the prophets endured immense suffering while patiently waiting for God's promises to be fulfilled, we are to do the same.

After telling us to look to the example of the prophets, James singles out a particular individual: Job. He says, "You have heard of the steadfastness of Job, and you have seen the purpose of the Lord, how the Lord is compassionate and merciful" (v. 11). Job's faithfulness in the midst of suffering teaches us several things. First, Satan accused Job of being faithful to God only because of God's blessings and protection (Job 1:6-12). Satan makes that same accusation against us today. Is our trust and love for God dependent on our circumstances? Or, like

Job, will we continue to bless the name of the Lord *despite* our circumstances? Second, even in the midst of our pain, God's presence meets us where we are. Just as God answered Job in his affliction, He will answer us. "Draw near to God and He will draw near to you" (James 4:8). Third, God not only restored what Job had lost but also gave him much more. Likewise, the reward that awaits us at the coming of the Lord if we remain faithful will be much more than what we've lost in this life. We trust in God's goodness in the midst of trials, knowing that He is compassionate and merciful.

James' statement on oaths in verse 12 seems a little out of place. But as Nystrom[1] points out, when this passage is viewed as yet another prohibition against improper speech, it fits in right here—especially when we consider it in contradistinction to the proper speech encouraged by James in the following section (prayer, singing praise, confession). James' teaching on oaths follows Yeshua's teaching in Matthew 5:34-37 almost verbatim. Like Yeshua, James is not prohibiting vows or oaths altogether. After all, the apostles continued to make vows and oaths (Acts 18:18; 21:23). And as Tim Hegg[2] points out, saying "yes" or "no," which both Yeshua and James tell us to do, was itself considered an oath, as expressed in the rabbinic literature (b.*Shavu'ot* 36a; b.*Bava Metzia* 49a). Both Yeshua's and James' point is that we should speak plainly and with integrity, with the full intention of keeping our word.

---

1 David Nystrom, *The NIV Application Commentary: James* (Grand Rapids, MI: Zondervan, 1997). EPUB: James 5:12-18, para 4.

2 Tim Hegg, *Commentary on the Gospel of Matthew Chapters 1-7* (Tacoma, WA: TorahResource, 2007) pp. 211-212

Gratitude: A Moral Mandate

The Bible is clear that being a Christian is more than just a one-time decision. Indeed, the fact that you've recited a prayer to receive Yeshua one time in your life doesn't mean that you're truly a follower of Messiah. For instance, how many New Year's resolutions are broken every year? Most people think they're being serious when they make a resolution to wake up extra early every day or exercise five times a week or whatever. But their seriousness, or lack thereof, is proven by their actions. In the same way, our decision to follow Messiah is proven by what we do. James says that faith without works is dead (2:17). John says that if you claim to know the Messiah but do not follow His commandments, then you are a liar (1 John 2:3-4). The point is this: If you claim to be a believer but that truth is not evident in your life, then you are not really a believer.

If we take God's Word seriously, then we need to make sure that we're actually practicing what we profess to believe. The apostle Paul says, "Examine yourselves, to see whether you are in the faith" (2 Corinthians 13:5). How do we know that we're in the faith? Well, are you walking in God's will or not? That's the question we have to ask ourselves. And with that in mind, it's important that we define what God's will actually is. The Bible has an answer for us:

> Rejoice always, pray without ceasing, give thanks in all circumstances; *for this is the will of God in Christ Jesus for you.* (1 Thessalonians 5:16-18, emphasis added)

According to Paul, God's will includes rejoicing, praying, and giving thanks. This can be summed up in one word: gratitude. Based on this passage, believers have a moral mandate to be grateful—to rejoice in His goodness, to pray, and give thanks to Him. Gratitude is not something that we can do with or without—it's fundamental to our walk as believers.

But why is gratitude so important to God? First, our gratitude honors God—and that's the purpose of our life! We are created to know God and bring Him glory. The psalmist declares, "The one who offers thanksgiving as his sacrifice glorifies me" (Psalm 50:23).

The opposite is also true. When we do *not* give thanks—when we are ungrateful—we *dishonor* God. Isn't this what we see time and time again after God delivered the Israelites from slavery in Egypt? You would think they would be grateful that they were saved from slavery, yet all they seem to do is complain and grumble—they're thirsty, hungry, they don't like Moses, etc. And while it's easy to look back at the Israelites and judge them, we often do the same thing, don't we? We complain about the very things we used to hope and pray for—our job, spouse, house, friends, church, etc. Complaining is the opposite of gratitude. In fact, ungrateful grumbling is so dishonoring to God that it incites His judgment:

> Do not grumble against one another, brothers, so that you may not be judged; behold, the Judge is standing at the door. (James 5:9)

Often the reason we're ungrateful is that we have a sense of entitlement. We think God owes us—like He's some kind of genie that we've summoned from a magic lamp and His purpose is to grant us wishes. We complain because we somehow think we deserve more and better than what we have. We've forgotten that what we actually deserve is to go to hell. However, rather than condemning us to hell like we deserve, God has mercy on us—and we can be grateful for that! Scripture says, "For by grace you have been saved through faith. And this is not your own doing; it is the gift of God" (Ephesians 2:8). God's grace is a gift. What do you say when someone gives you a gift? "Thank you." God has given us the greatest gift in His Son, Yeshua the Messiah. Therefore, how can we *not* be grateful?

A second reason gratitude is important is that it causes us to appreciate what we have rather than long for what we don't have. Nothing is wrong with wishing for better circumstances, a bigger home to fit your growing family, a raise at work, etc. But you cannot be grateful for something you don't already have—it's impossible. And if your sole focus is on attaining more money, a better job, a bigger house, etc., you'll never be satisfied even when you get those things. Solomon wrote, "He who loves money will not be satisfied with money, nor he who loves wealth with his income; this also is vanity" (Ecclesiastes 5:10).

A third reason gratitude is important is that it helps us grow in faith and steadfastness. Even in times of profound pain, grief, and loss, we can still be grateful that we have Yeshua. We can still be grateful that the promises of God are true and that His justice will prevail. Choosing gratitude in times of trial helps us remain humble and trust in God's goodness, even when all hope seems lost. Paul said we are to "give thanks in all circumstances" (1 Thessalonians 5:18)—especially difficult circumstances.

A fourth reason gratitude is important is that it makes the world better. When we're feeling grateful, we're automatically more inclined to be nicer to people. We feel joyful and generous and humble. The opposite is also true: ingratitude makes the world worse. When we're feeling ungrateful, we're automatically more inclined to be unkind to people. We treat the waitress at the restaurant with disrespect. We complain and grumble, making everyone else around us miserable.

Since gratitude is a moral mandate, that entails we have a choice in the matter. It's not always an easy choice, but we must decide to be grateful daily, especially when the feeling doesn't come naturally. God is worthy of our thanks in all circumstances. Charles Spurgeon puts it well:

> Here is a standing reason for thanksgiving. Although we may not always be healthy, nor always prosperous, yet God is always good, and, therefore, there is always a sufficient argument for giving thanks unto Jehovah. That he is a good God essentially, that he cannot be otherwise than good, should be a fountain out of which the richest praises should perpetually flow.[3]

Don't Be A Flake

The Torah commands us to keep our promises (e.g. Numbers 30:2). This is the duty of every follower of Messiah. Yeshua and James taught that we should be such a people of integrity that making an elaborate oath would be completely unnecessary—we don't have to sell ourselves because our simple "yes" or "no" is trusted and sufficient (Matthew 5:34-37; James 5:12). Why is keeping our promises so important? Because we bear God's image. And since God always keeps His word, we must keep our word as well.

A "flake" is someone who makes promises but doesn't follow through with them. They are unreliable. They are the people who make plans to be somewhere but never show up. And even if they have the decency to inform you that they won't be there, they'll usually just send a text message at the last minute saying that "something came up." The flaky person cannot commit to anything.

---

3 Charles H. Spurgeon, *Commentary on Psalms 118:4.* "Spurgeon's Verse Expositions of the Bible." www.studylight.org. Accessed 12/19/2018

Ultimately, flakiness comes down to a lack of love and consideration for others, which breaks the second greatest commandment to "love your neighbor as yourself" (James 2:8). If people truly loved their neighbor as themselves, they wouldn't be flaky. That's because everyone who has ever dealt with a flaky person knows how utterly disrespectful and frustrating it can be.

When we who claim to follow the God of Israel flake out on others—when we break God's commandment to keep our promises—we profane the name of God. Believers are called to be "imitators of God" (Ephesians 5:1). Is your life a representation of God's faithfulness, or by your actions do you make God out to be an unreliable flake?

CHAPTER 18

PRAY AND CONFESS

Is anyone among you suffering? Let him pray. Is anyone cheerful? Let him sing praise. Is anyone among you sick? Let him call for the elders of the church, and let them pray over him, anointing him with oil in the name of the Lord. And the prayer of faith will save the one who is sick, and the Lord will raise him up. And if he has committed sins, he will be forgiven. Therefore, confess your sins to one another and pray for one another, that you may be healed. The prayer of a righteous person has great power as it is working. Elijah was a man with a nature like ours, and he prayed fervently that it might not rain, and for three years and six months it did not rain on the earth. Then he prayed again, and heaven gave rain, and the earth bore its fruit.

James 5:13-18

As James draws his epistle to a close, he gives his readers some final pastoral counsel: "Is anyone among you suffering? Let him pray" (v. 13). James began his epistle with instruction on how to handle trials, and he concludes with this same theme. James makes it clear that a faithful life of service and devotion to the Messiah will come with trials and suffering. In those moments, it is difficult to believe in God's goodness, but we must not succumb to despair. In the midst of the storm, we have hope in the promise of Messiah—that He has overcome the world: "In the world you will have tribulation. But take heart; I have overcome the world" (John 16:33). Therefore, our response to suffering is faithful endurance and prayer.

James then addresses those in the community who are cheerful: "Is anyone cheerful? Let him sing praise" (v. 13). It's important to note that James is not referring to those who are feeling happy-go-lucky because life is good. In this context, being cheerful means having courage in the midst of trials. McKnight writes:

> This term evokes enthusiasm, courage, and a confident faith and these often in the context of stress [...] The contrast here is not between suffering and the good life but within a group where everyone is undergoing persecution or suffering, some of whom are struggling and others who have taken courage.[1]

James' instruction for the "cheerful" is to sing praise. We worship and thank God for giving us the strength to endure trials. Whether we are suffering or cheerful, James' desire is that we look to God. Our natural inclination when we go through trials is to give in to doubt (James 1:6), fighting (James 4:1-2), and complaining (James 5:9). James teaches us to trust in God's goodness and pursue Him in faith through prayer and praise.

Next, James turns his attention to those who are sick: "Is anyone among you sick? Let him call for the elders of the church, and let them pray over him, anointing him with oil in the name of the Lord" (v. 14). The Greek word translated "sick," *astheneo*, often refers to physical illness, but it can also denote emotional or even spiritual weakness (Acts 20:35; 2 Corinthians 12:10; Romans 5:6). McKnight argues that James is most likely referring to someone who is physically ill and possibly bedridden:

> Furthermore, this third condition provokes James to mention not only elders and anointing but also the need for strong faith

---

1 Scot McKnight, *The New International Commentary of the New Testament: The Letter of James* (Grand Rapids, MI: Wm. B. Eerdmans Publishing Co., 2011) p. 433

> and righteous people praying for the person. This evidence suggests this person is seriously and physically ill, perhaps near death, though the terms are expansive enough that they might include a number of issues.[2]

James instructs the sick to call for the elders of the community to come, pray for them, and anoint them with oil. In addition to serving a symbolic role of consecrating a person to the Lord's care, oil was used for medicinal purposes. For instance, the good Samaritan used oil to treat the wounds of the injured man on the road (Luke 10:34). The point to draw from this verse is that we are not to suffer alone. The community is to surround those who are sick, comfort them, and pray for them. Yeshua said that when we visit and care for the sick, it is as if we are doing it to Him (Matthew 25:36). Believers, especially elders and leaders, ought to visit and care for the sick in their community.

After teaching that the elders are to visit the sick, anoint them, and pray for them, James says, "And the prayer of faith will save the one who is sick, and the Lord will raise him up. And if he has committed sins, he will be forgiven" (v. 15). Just as we ask for God's wisdom in faith (James 1:6), prayers for healing must likewise be in faith—that is, a complete trust in God. When the elders pray in faith, the sick person can be expected to be made well. (This certainly isn't a guarantee, though, as we will explore later.) He also says their sins will be forgiven. Though sickness is often connected with sin (e.g. John 5:14), the Scriptures certainly do not teach that sickness is always the result of sin (e.g. John 9:2-3). Nevertheless, James teaches that healing from illness—regardless of the cause—can occur through confession and prayer: "Therefore, confess your sins to one another and pray for

---

2 Ibid., p. 435

one another, that you may be healed. The prayer of a righteous person has great power as it is working" (v. 16). While this passage still specifically has the elders in view, it is applied more broadly to the whole community. Communal confession of sins is an important practice throughout the Scriptures (Ezra 10; Matthew 3:6; Acts 19:18). We could perhaps say that "coming clean" by confessing our sins to trusted leaders or friends within the community is part of what it means to find healing and relief from emotional and spiritual turmoil:

> For when I kept silent, my bones wasted away through my groaning all day long. For day and night your hand was heavy upon me; my strength was dried up as by the heat of summer. I acknowledged my sin to you, and I did not cover my iniquity; I said, "I will confess my transgressions to the Lord," and you forgave the iniquity of my sin. (Psalm 32:3-5)

As an example of the power of prayer, James brings up the prophet Elijah (vv. 17-18). Elijah was a man "with a nature like ours." He was fully human like us. Therefore, James encourages us to view Elijah as an example of a righteous, prayerful person through whom God worked miracles. What was possible with Elijah is also possible with us. James says, "Then he prayed again, and heaven gave rain, and the earth bore its fruit" (v. 18). Just as Elijah's prayers resulted in healing on the earth, the prayers of a righteous person can bring healing to the sick.

Why Sing?

The Westminster Shorter Catechism states that man's chief end is to glorify God and to enjoy him forever.[3] Indeed, our purpose is

---

3 Westminster Shorter Catechism (1674). www.ccel.org.

to honor God with our lives, and we fulfill that purpose in many different ways. We glorify God by our obedience and faithful service to Him on earth. We glorify Him by drawing near to Him through our study of the Scriptures, learning more about Him, and growing in our love and affection for Him. We glorify Him by caring for the "least of these." We glorify Him by the spreading of the Gospel, bringing people from every tribe and tongue to the throne of God (Revelation 7:9-10). Moreover, as the Scriptures testify, we glorify God by singing praise.

Psalm 30:4 tells us to "sing praises to the Lord, O you his saints, and give thanks to his holy name." Psalm 46:6 says, "Sing praises to God, sing praises! Sing praises to our King, sing praises!" If we take Scripture to be instruction on how we ought to live, wouldn't that include this exhortation from the Psalms to sing to the Lord? (Interestingly, the book of Psalms is itself a collection of songs, which shows us how passionate God is about music—He sovereignly chose a giant collection of song lyrics to be included in the holy Scriptures!) Even our Messiah Yeshua Himself sang hymns with His disciples (Matthew 26:30). And the apostles also instructed us to sing to the Lord (James 5:13; Colossians 3:16).

Singing to God is clearly important in Scripture. But why? For one, singing songs is a way to unite the community of Messiah. When everyone is singing the same words—declaring the same biblical truths at the same time—it has a powerful unifying affect for the body of Messiah. Yeshua's prayer just prior to His arrest, shortly before being crucified, included a fervent desire that His followers would be one (John 17:21-22). Certainly the Lord is blessed by our singing together with one voice, praising the one true God.

Music also tends to have a powerful emotional impact on us. Worship is not only studying God's word and keeping His commandments but also engaging Him on an emotional level. Craig Keener writes:

> Much of the worship in the Bible involves singing, and singing involves emotions (and our body) as well as intellect. We should know and celebrate God with our whole person. While too many Christians neglect to serve God with the mind, others cultivate only their minds and neglect the emotional aspects of worship.[4]

Finally, music and singing help us to memorize important biblical truth. God gave us music and melodies as a way to remember who He is and what He's done. When the Israelites were saved from the Egyptians, the first thing they did was sing a song (Exodus 15). They wanted to always remember how amazing and powerful and loving their God is! And how much more of a reason do *we* have to sing to sing praises to our God? We have been delivered from the slavery of sin and death by the Messiah Yeshua. He is worthy to be praised!

When God Doesn't Heal

James teaches us that when we pray in faith for the sick to be healed, we can expect that they will be healed (James 5:15). However, while many of us have witnessed miraculous healing happen on occasion, it seems that most of the time the sick are not healed when we pray for them. Why? Is it due to a lack of faith? Is some

---

4 Craig Keener, *Gift Giver: The Holy Spirit for Today* (Grand Rapids, MI: Baker Academic, 2002), p. 32

unconfessed sin preventing God from healing the person? Or is there another reason?

Scripture is clear that God is about life and health for His people. Moses exhorted us to obey God and "choose life" (Deuteronomy 30:19). One of the blessings for obedience is that God will take away sicknesses and diseases (Deuteronomy 7:15). It seems clear that God's will is that we walk in His ways for His glory *and* our good. Furthermore, when we get to the New Testament, we see that Yeshua was moved by compassion to heal the sick (Matthew 9:36; 14:14; 20:34; Mark 1:41; Luke 7:13), demonstrating that life and healing are part of God's very character. He has a profound concern for the hurting, and thus He's deeply moved to respond to them. That's His heart. And it's on the basis of that deep desire of God's heart that Yeshua commissioned His disciples to continue the mission of bringing the Kingdom to earth, which includes laying hands on the sick that they would be healed (Mark 16:18). This is a sign that will accompany "all those who believe" (Mark 16:17), not just the original apostles (Acts 8:7; James 5:15). Additionally, healing is listed as one of the spiritual gifts for the edification of the Church (1 Corinthians 12:9).

Every Bible believer should agree that God can and does heal. And every Bible believer should agree that life and health, not death and sickness, are God's ideal will for His people—after all, in the world to come, all His people will be healed and death and pain will be no more (Revelation 21:4). This future world has already broken into our reality through Yeshua's resurrection, thus we can expect divine healing to occur even now. But that does *not* entail that God will *always* heal the sick *in this life*.

Prosperity preachers claim that if you just have enough "faith," which is often incorrectly defined as ascending to a certain level of psychological certainty, God will *always* bring about supernatural healing. It's supposedly guaranteed because Christ purchased our healing when He died and rose from the grave. But if that were true, then there can be no exceptions. Judging by the experience of most believers today, divine healing is far from a 100% guaranteed result of prayer. (In fact, divine healing actually tends to be the exception!) While Scripture is full of examples of divine healing, we also see some exceptions in Scripture too. For instance, Paul left Trophimus sick in Miletus (2 Timothy 4:20) and instructed Timothy to drink a little wine to ease his "frequent ailments" (1 Timothy 5:23). Why didn't Paul simply pray that they be healed? Should we assume that Paul lacked faith?

The prosperity preacher might claim that God did not heal someone because of unconfessed sin. However, they should be careful making an accusation like that. The logical implication of their claim is that a person *must* be in sin if they are sick. But Yeshua corrected His disciples for making the assumption that a man's blindness was because of sin (John 9:1-3). Moreover, God Himself said that Job, who suffered terrible misfortunes, including painful sores all of his body (Job 2:7), was a "blameless and upright man" (Job 1:8). After Job's friends accused him of having some secret sin in his life, the Lord sharply rebuked them for their errant assumption (Job 42:7-9). The simple fact is that many godly and faithful people have suffered due to illness and have even died young. God didn't heal them.

How then do we reconcile passages like James 5:15, which seem to promise divine healing, with other passages of Scripture and our experiences? One solution might be to look at that passage as a proverb instead of as a promise. That is to say, divine healing does happen, and we can reasonably expect it to happen as the Church prays in faith for the sick, but it is not promised to happen in every situation every time. This is simply the nature of our fallen world. For instance, obedience to God's commandments is said to bring blessing, but as we learn from the books of Ecclesiastes and Job, righteous living is not a guarantee against pain and suffering. Nevertheless, when we do live a life of obedience, we can generally expect the result to be life and blessing. Scripture says that when we train up our children in the way of the Lord, they will not depart from the faith when they get older (Proverbs 22:6). But many children who were raised in godly homes *do* abandon their faith when they get older. Nevertheless, parents who train their children in the way of the Lord can generally expect them to remain faithful to God in adulthood. "Excellent" wives, according to Proverbs 31, can reasonably expect their husbands to praise them (Proverbs 31:28). But many husbands are jerks regardless of how excellent their wife is. Nevertheless, excellent wives can generally expect praise from their husbands. You get the picture.

James' instruction to pray for the sick is something that we apply with hope and expectation that God will act. But we also remember that we live in a fallen, broken world. The Messiah's Kingdom, in which sickness and death will be abolished, has not yet fully been made manifest. Our guaranteed healing won't take place until Yeshua returns. Until then, we patiently endure trials, including sickness, trusting that God's ways are higher than ours. We give thanks in the midst of our affliction, knowing that God uses our suffering to conform us into the image of His Son. We comfort those who are hurting and mourn with those who mourn. And indeed, we also pray, expecting that it's God's will to heal. He will heal some in this life and not others, but we still pray. Until the Kingdom comes in fullness, we will just have to trust God in the midst of that unresolved tension.

CHAPTER 19

BRING BACK THE WANDERER

My brothers, if anyone among you wanders from the truth and someone brings him back, let him know that whoever brings back a sinner from his wandering will save his soul from death and will cover a multitude of sins.

James 5:19-20

James concludes his letter with an exhortation to the Messianic community to bring back those who have wandered from the truth. Whatever the backslidden individual has done—perhaps they're guilty of the very sins that James outlines in his epistle—followers of Yeshua have a responsibility to attempt to lovingly correct and restore them. James equates restoring the backslidden sinner to saving their soul from death! He also says that it covers "a multitude of sins." Yeshua's parable about leaving the ninety-nine sheep to retrieve the one that went astray perhaps forms the backdrop of James' instructions here (Matthew 18:10-14).

We often think of the English word *wander* in the sense of something accidental or done in ignorance, like a toddler wandering off and getting into something they aren't supposed to. According to Nystrom, the implication of the "wandering" in this passage is not wholly innocent: "The wanderer may understand that the path chosen is a deviant path; or if the wanderer has pursued the path accidentally or unconsciously, those teaching and practicing this error are certainly conscious of it as different from the truth that they know."[1] Peter uses the same word (*planao*) to describe a deliberate decision to walk in sin: "Forsaking the right way, they have gone astray [*planao*]. They have followed the way of Balaam, the son of Beor, who loved gain from wrongdoing" (2 Peter 2:15).

In either case, James says the wanderer has wandered "from the truth." Walking in truth, as James has made especially clear, is not only having the right beliefs but also living out those beliefs. That's why the one who wanders from the truth is called a "sinner"—they have chosen to turn away from doing the word of truth (James 1:18, 22-25). Similar to what Paul commands in Galatians 6:1, James is instructing believers to lovingly confront those who have fallen into sin in hopes that they would repent. Restoration of the wanderer will also "cover a multitude of sins" (Proverbs 10:12), bringing about forgiveness and resolution. The act of lovingly correcting a sinner and bringing them back restores the wanderer to a right relationship not only with God but also the community, which is the goal.

James here echoes Yeshua's powerful message of forgiveness and reconciliation. Yeshua said His mission was to "seek and save the lost" (Luke 19:10). Whether the lost person is someone who has wandered from the truth or someone who has never followed the truth to begin with, believers are to be like Yeshua—we are to go to the lost and bring them to the cross. We are to share with them the hope we all have in the Gospel. Forgiveness and healing are available when we simply turn from our sins and accept God's invitation to come home.

---

1 David Nystrom, The NIV Application Commentary: James (Grand Rapids, MI: Zondervan, 1997). EPUB: James 5:19-20, para 6.

Returning What Was Lost

The Torah commands us to return lost items to their owners. This law is known as *hashavat aveida*, "returning lost objects," and it's found in Deuteronomy:

> You shall not see your brother's ox or his sheep going astray and ignore them. You shall take them back to your brother. And if he does not live near you and you do not know who he is, you shall bring it home to your house, and it shall stay with you until your brother seeks it. Then you shall restore it to him. And you shall do the same with his donkey or with his garment, or with any lost thing of your brother's, which he loses and you find; you may not ignore it. (Deuteronomy 22:1-3)

What can we learn from this commandment? First, we are to go *out of our way* to restore what was lost. If we have an opportunity to help, we cannot ignore it. This commandment is ultimately an expression of the royal law to love our neighbor (James 2:8). Love looks out for others in the community. The idea of "finders keepers, losers weepers" is a selfish attitude and simply not biblical.

Second, this law applies not only to our brothers but also to those we might consider our enemies! This passage in Deuteronomy is a reiteration of a commandment previously given in Exodus, which says, "If you meet your *enemy's* ox or his donkey going astray, you shall bring it back to him" (Exodus 23:4, emphasis added). What's the significance of this? Quite simply, we cannot allow our emotions or hurt feelings to dictate whether or not we do the right thing. Even if someone has offended us or doesn't like us, we are still to go out of our way to help them. We are to show love and compassion toward everyone, including our enemies. After all, didn't our Father in heaven show *us* compassion when we were considered *His* enemy? Yeshua said, "Do good to those who hate you" (Luke 6:27). We do not have the authority to exempt ourselves from loving our neighbor just because it's someone we don't like!

Third, we can draw a principle from this commandment that can be applied beyond mere physical objects. For instance, if we know someone who has "lost" their faith in God and has gone astray, we are to go out of our way to try to restore them (James 5:19-20). We should have a loving concern for those struggling with doubt and should look for ways to encourage them. We can invite them to church or to our home for *erev Shabbat* so they can experience God's presence through our hospitality, ask us questions, and maybe reclaim their faith.

This principle could perhaps be extended even further. For instance, if someone is depressed and feels that they've "lost" their sense of value—maybe they just had a relationship fall apart and they're going through a difficult time—we should go out of our way to encourage them and remind them how loved they are. Moreover, many of us have Christian friends who've "lost" something of tremendous value to their faith—the Sabbath and feast days! Keeping the principle of this commandment would therefore entail restoring these biblical commandments to our Christian brothers. We can invite them to a Sabbath service at our congregation or to a Passover seder. We can have a Bible study with them and go through the Scriptures to show them that God still cares about those parts of His word. Maybe they'll see the value of what they've lost and want to start keeping these things.

We as followers of Yeshua need to reclaim this important commandment that seems to have been lost in our culture. May we have a concern for our neighbor's property and make sure lost money, items, etc., are returned to them—it's an expression of love for our neighbor, the second greatest commandment (Matthew 22:39). And may we be willing to go out of our way to restore not only physical items to our neighbor but also the deeper things they might've lost as well. This is the law of *hashavat aveida.*

Restoring the Wanderer

In His parable of the Lost Sheep, Yeshua expresses the heart of God toward His wayward people with the imagery of a shepherd who intentionally seeks and rescues his sheep that have gone astray (Matthew 18:10-14). As image bearers of God, we ought to have that same heart for the lost sheep—that is, those who have wandered away from the truth into sin. Just as the flock is not whole when one sheep goes missing, our communities are not whole when even one person abandons the ways of Messiah. And just as the shepherd rejoices over finding the lost sheep, we are to have that same sentiment when a brother repents of his sin. Yeshua said, "So it is not the will of my Father who is in heaven that one of these little ones should perish" (Matthew 18:14). Thus, we likewise must not resent those who wander but earnestly hope that they will repent, receive forgiveness, and be reconciled.

After His parable, Yeshua gives instructions on how to lovingly address sin within the community. Situations in which someone must be approached about sin are always sensitive, which is why Yeshua preceded these instructions by expressing God's compassion for the sinner. In addition, immediately following these instructions, Yeshua gives another parable on the value of forgiveness (Matthew 18:21-35), further demonstrating the utmost care and mercy with which we should approach those who've wandered into sin. Here is what Yeshua says about confronting a brother in sin:

> If your brother sins against you, go and tell him his fault, between you and him alone. If he listens to you, you have gained your brother. But if he does not listen, take one or two others along with you, that every charge may be established by the evidence of two or three witnesses. If he refuses to listen to them, tell it to the church. And if he refuses to listen even to the church, let him be to you as a Gentile and a tax collector. (Matthew 18:15-17)

As we can see, the goal of these instructions is for restoration—bringing a lost sheep back to the fold. The goal is to gain your brother back because you deeply love them and you're concerned for their spiritual health. Therefore, reproving your brother begins in private: "If your brother sins against you, go and tell him his fault, *between you and him alone.*"

Being confronted about your sins is an uncomfortable and embarrassing situation, hence why it should be handled in private. It should also be handled gently and compassionately: "Brothers, if anyone is caught in any transgression, you who are spiritual should restore him in a spirit of gentleness" (Galatians 6:1). A gentle reproof in private mitigates the embarrassment and therefore the potential of the erring brother to get defensive and defiant. Scripture commands us to speak the truth in love (Ephesians 4:15). The fact that the Bible specifies truth spoken "in love" is an indication that there are other ways to speak the truth—one could speak the truth with uncaring arrogance, for instance. Truth is truth, but how we deliver it makes all the difference. People are more willing to listen and receive the truth when it's delivered with love and gentleness. And since the goal is to gain your brother, we do well to handle these situations with prayer and the utmost sensitivity.

Nevertheless, occasionally people will refuse to humble themselves and repent even when their sin is clearly made known to them beyond dispute. In such a scenario, Yeshua instructs us to "take one or two others along with you, that every charge may be established by the evidence of two or three witnesses." Yeshua quotes the Torah here (e.g. Deuteronomy 19:15). The Torah states that at least two or three witnesses are required to establish a charge of sin. If the brother has refused to repent of his sin, the matter moves beyond private correction to a matter of legal consequence potentially resulting in removal from the community. According to Tim Hegg, the witnesses function not necessarily as additional voices of reproof but as witnesses that the person had been confronted with proof of their transgression:

> The witnesses are there to verify that the erring brother has been reproved and to give testimony to his response. Since his failure to heed the second reproof might eventuate in his being 'cut off' from the community, such a severe measure would require more than one witness.[2]

If the brother in sin refuses to repent, despite having been confronted in private and then again before additional witnesses, the matter is then handed over to the leaders[3] of the community who "tell it to the church." This, again, is done with the hope that the erring brother will turn from their sin and be restored. But in

---

2 Tim Hegg, *Commentary on the Gospel of Matthew Chapters 13-18* (Tacoma, WA: TorahResource, 2010) p. 788

3 Ibid: "Though the present text does not give procedural details, it seems certain that after refusing to respond appropriately to the first and second approaches, the matter is given over to the leaders of the assembly (elders / overseers) who then must make the matter known to the community as a whole" (p. 790).

addition to that, it serves as a warning to the local community of the potential threat posed by the erring brother who is now acting in rebellion. If he refuses to listen to the community, Yeshua says to "let him be to you as a Gentile and a tax collector." That is to say, the community as a whole trusts the ruling of their congregational leadership and thus excludes the brother from the community in hopes that the shame of their exclusion might eventually lead to repentance and restoration.

While many Christians today might look at these instructions as unloving and harsh, nothing could be further from the truth. Matters of Church discipline are not to be taken lightly. Moreover, these situations are followed with the intended goal of forgiveness and restoration. Even if the matter is taken all the way to the point of the person being excluded, the hope is that God would bring them to a place of repentance so they might rejoin the community. These are certainly difficult biblical instructions that must be applied prayerfully and with godly wisdom. Ultimately, congregational leaders have the tough job of making the final difficult decision of whether or not to exclude an unrepentant sinner from the community. The rest of the congregation needs to pray for their leaders to have wisdom and that love and mercy would guide them. Then they must trust their leaders and stand with them in support of their decision.

Concluding Thoughts

James' letter ends abruptly after his comments on restoring the wayward sinner, which perhaps suggests that he wants to leave his readers with that lingering imperative to repent. May we take James' exhortation to heart.

Have you wavered in your alliance to God despite His abounding goodness? Have you given in to sinful desires, bringing forth death to yourself and those around you? Have you been a religious hypocrite, claiming to have faith in Messiah but neglecting to actually live out His teachings? Have you neglected to care for the poor, the widow, and the orphan? Have you slandered your brothers and sisters, causing strife within your community? Have you run over others in your quest for personal honor and self-fulfillment? Have you hijacked God's authority by speaking evil against your brothers and sisters and condemning them? Have you put God in second place to your own selfish agenda?

If that is you, James says to repent and be restored! God will forgive you and receive you. May He be glorified as we all turn back from our wandering and pursue a life of faith that works—living out the law of liberty in accordance with Scripture.

ABOUT DAVID WILBER

I am first and foremost a follower of Yeshua the Messiah. In addition to my books, *When Faith Works: Living Out the Law of Liberty According to James* and *A Christian Guide to the Biblical Feasts*, I've written several theological and devotional articles available on various Messianic and Christian websites. I've also spoken at a number of Christian/Messianic churches and conferences throughout the United States and serve as a regular Bible teacher and writer for multiple congregations and ministries, such as Freedom Hill Community, Founded in Truth Fellowship, and 119 Ministries.

One of my passions is to minister to God's people by helping them rediscover the beauty and value of God's Torah. Why? Because Torah observance is an important part of the life and message of our Messiah. It was prophesied that the Messiah would "elevate the Torah and make it honorable" (Isaiah 42:21). The New Covenant established by Yeshua is intended to write the Torah on our hearts through the work of the Holy Spirit (Jeremiah 31:33). Yeshua upheld every dot and iota of the Torah and taught us how to apply it in light of the New Covenant (Matthew 5:17-20). The word *Christian* literally means "follower of Christ." As such, Christians are to walk as Yeshua walked (1 John 2:6). Since Yeshua kept and taught the Torah, it is appropriate for us to do the same.

Another passion of mine is to assist believers in being able to give an answer to anyone who asks about the hope within them (1 Peter 3:15). We are morally responsible to believe, proclaim, and defend the truth and refute falsehoods (Jude 1:3). A branch of theology known as apologetics is devoted to such a task. Therefore, much of my teaching and writing is designed to help believers engage in apologetics so they can confidently answer objections from critics of Christianity and the Bible.

While I certainly don't think of myself as any kind of expert scholar or theologian, I don't believe that God gave me these passions for no reason. And if I can be of service to the body of Messiah, I want to do what I can to help for the glory of God. My plan, therefore, is simply to continue developing resources. In addition to this book, I have a library of articles and videos available for free on my website (www.davidwilber.me). Feel free to connect with me there and on social media. If you'd like to invite me to speak at your congregation or conference, you can contact me through my website.

I hope you were blessed by this book. Thanks for reading, and may the Lord bless you and draw near to you as you draw near to Him. Blessings and Shalom!

Made in the USA
Lexington, KY
27 February 2019